by William Gibson

WINTER CROOK (*poems*)

DINNY AND THE WITCHES (*play*)

A CRY OF PLAYERS (*play*)

THE COBWEB (*novel*)

TWO FOR THE SEESAW (*play*)

THE SEESAW LOG (*chronicle*)

THE MIRACLE WORKER (*play*)

A MASS FOR THE DEAD (*chronicle & poems*)

AMERICAN PRIMITIVE (*play*)

A SEASON IN HEAVEN (*chronicle*)

THE BODY & THE WHEEL (*play*)

THE BUTTERFINGERS ANGEL, MARY AND JOSEPH, HEROD
THE NUT, AND THE SLAUGHTER OF 12 HIT CAROLS IN A
PEAR TREE (*play*)

GOLDA (*play*)

SHAKESPEARE'S GAME (*criticism*)

with Clifford Odets

GOLDEN BOY (*musical*)

*Notes on How to Turn a Phoenix
Into Ashes*

G O L D A

Notes on How to Turn a Phoenix Into Ashes

THE STORY OF THE STAGE PRODUCTION, WITH THE TEXT, OF

GOLDA

by William Gibson

NEW YORK *Atheneum* 1978

Library of Congress Cataloging in Publication Data
Gibson, William, date
    Golda.
    Play.
    1. Meir, Golda Mabovitz, 1898–   ——Drama.
PS3513.I2824G6   812'.5'4   77–15889
ISBN 0–689–10876–1

FOR

the Lady herself

NATURALLY

Contents

*Notes on How to Turn a Phoenix
Into Ashes*

GOLDA

Notes on How to Turn a Phoenix Into Ashes

A FEW FRIENDS, including my publisher, have suggested that a history of this play might be more—they didn't say "even" more—interesting than the play itself. I am not of that view, though in a history of three hundred pages I might justify it; I will content myself with thirty.

1.

I did anticipate that a year given to such a play would be a memorable one in my life; it was a big reason for my saying yes when Philip Langner of the Theatre Guild first phoned to invite me to try it. I said no. I knew little of Golda Meir and wasn't sure I could take time to learn more, my first piece of opacity in this venture; but I had spent three emotional weeks in Israel some years before, carried a certain passion for it in me, and Langner said, "Oh, then you must write it!—this play isn't to make money, it's for humanity." Such a sentiment was so unexpected from a producer that it confused me, and a month later—May, 1976—I found myself in New York, sitting in a hotel suite with him and Golda.

I never called her by anything but her first name, but she awed me. A grandmother half my height, mas-

sive as a boulder, she exuded a natural power without lifting her pinky; she did lift her eyebrows, said, "Stories, stories—" and told a couple of harrowing honeys, with humor, and I was hooked, by history, vanity, and the duty to court larger risks. I was there to explain that the only play I glimpsed in her autobiography was one I doubted I could write. I said I'd therefore like to take a crack at it, but couldn't peel her life away from that of the state she had helped found, and my play would be about the state via the life; if she or Langner wanted a different play, they should ask a different playwright. Nobody demurring, we went our separate ways, Golda to a tour of speaking engagements and I to several weeks of reading my eyes blurry.

Glimpsed was the word. I had in sight the first minute of the script and the last, with nothing in between but a hope that the Yom Kippur War—the salient drama of Golda's prime ministership, which indeed ended it—might give me an aspic in which to suspend a variety of fruits. It was the fruits I was after, and the reading was preliminary; the real research was in talking to people, her relatives, friends, enemies, coworkers of a lifetime. I began the interviewing in this country, and in August flew to Israel.

Changing to an El Al plane in the Zurich airport, I waited in a queue patrolled by Israeli soldiers with machine-guns, and saw I was entering a country under siege; two days later, four died in a terrorist attack on El Al at Istanbul.

2.

Solitude is the food of my life, but for the next three months I rode busses to the spartan homes, offices, restaurants of that unchic land and interviewed Israelis —three, four, five a day—and it was a feast.

There is no small talk in Israel, one word about the weather leads instantly into tales of life and death in the extermination camps and the wars, and no survivor without a twist of humor, the tragic mask reversed; it's like being in a Russian novel. I am speaking of the older generation, with its sense of moral burden and pride in progress. The young I met, like ours, are into arts and crafts, despise technology, envy the earthy simplicity they see in Bedouins, who are their Indians, and think their politicians a bit absurd. I thought them extraordinarily gifted, and with the help of Golda's assistant, Lou Kaddar, had entree to all. I ran a gamut of diplomats, bodyguards, Knesset members, rabbis, generals, chauffeurs, educators, secret-service directors, journalists, jurists, secretaries, doctors, anyone with news of Golda; I ate with her son, her daughter, her niece, her in-laws, her grandchildren, and—for good measure—with a few Arabs on the wrong side of Jerusalem, who almost talked me out of the play; I went from the elegant villa of Abba Eban, who presented me with his books and recorded speeches, to the compact kitchen of a manicurist Mancy, a numeral from Auschwitz who trimmed and buffed my nails as she did Golda's; and the one refusal to see me was by secretary over the phone, "General Dayan says no."

Golda herself was more indifferent than uncoopera-

tive, always booked, and in early September I phoned
her at home; I said I'd be leaving in a month, I needed
six or seven sessions with her.

I heard an instant "Oh no!" and could feel her scowl.
I said, "Did you think I could do it with less?"
Silence.
She said flatly, "So you're serving notice."
I said, scared, "Well—not serving notice, but—"
She said, "I'll call you Monday."

Lou Kaddar, a skeptic on everything, assured me she
would not. I said I believed Golda, and was willing to
bet a pound on it, about a dime; Lou said that was
no bet, it should be something significant. Like what?
—a bottle of wine. The best Israeli wine is a Cabernet
Sauvignon that costs two dollars, and I said she was on.

Tuesday I had the wine, and thereafter I saw Golda
whenever I could squeeze into her car and schedule.
I attended her at public ceremonies, and talked with
her in her little home in Ramat Aviv, in hotels on her
travels, in Lou's flat in Jerusalem; and with my wife—
who visited in the middle of my sojourn, and put in
a good word for me—I spent a long weekend en famille
in the Negev kibbutz which keeps a two-room nest for
Golda next to her daughter's. "Protectsia," said Golda,
meaning pull. It was not data I needed from her
but a sense of her flavor, and a good bit of dialogue
I took fresh off her tongue.

I was told fifty times she was "no intellectual," saw
everything simply in black and white, but had the gift
for going straight to the heart of any problem; I saw
it myself. Riding in her car between Tel Aviv and
Jerusalem, I confided to her my misgivings about writ-

ing imagined dialogue between her and her dead husband, she would hate it.

"Look," she said, "there are two places you'll have
to write dialogue. One is Milwaukee, when I decide
to come to Palestine, the other is Jerusalem, when I
left him."

I thought this ill-considered, it was ad lib, she barely
a theatregoer and I a professional playwright who after
weeks of thought had no idea yet how the structure
would unfold; but four months later, done, I saw those
were the two places I'd written the dialogue for.

Not all the stories I heard were flattering—a Knesset
member said, "The last thing we need is a paean to the
old guard"—and some were so hostile that to one
American-born interviewee I said, "Listen, I need a
heroine!" But the bulk of the testimony was respectful,
often loving, and those who had been at her side during
the Yom Kippur War were most affirmative. "Golda
was terrific," said a very tough general, "I salute her."
But in all the interviews I felt faintly fraudulent; busy
people were being generous and gracious to me for the
sake of a play I had no focus on, maybe couldn't write
at all, and more than once wished could be cancelled
by some worldwide disaster not my fault.

By the middle of October I was saturated, and rest-
less to begin. I holed up alone in a hospice—holed up
is hardly accurate, I worked in the sun on a rooftop with
an immense view of the Old City of Jerusalem—and
wrote the first eight minutes of dialogue. I saw the play
was in me, not in Golda, stuffed everything into my
backpack, and flew home.

3.

The idea of putting onstage a simulacrum of a living personage familiar to all the world—Golda said drily we "would make her famous"—was bizarre enough, and made interesting demands on a writer; but it was not what I intended the play to be about.

Later a critic doing a piece asked me whether it wouldn't have been a better play "if you were Jewish," which I thought a dopey question; I said yes, if I were Jewish and more talented. And added, it was written by a Christian who "carries in his consciousness two thousand years of history in which the crucified figure is that of the Jews." I am a recidivous Bible reader, and my first act after visiting Israel years before had been to read again its opening five books, known to all Jews as the Torah. It is one of the two pillars of western civilization, and of great pertinence to Americans: when in 1634 John Cotton drew up a code of laws for the six hundred souls of Boston he based it on Leviticus, a living current in the mind of that other Bostonian, John Adams, when in the next century he devised the constitution of Massachusetts on which that of the nation is modelled. Like anyone of sense, I saw the history of Israel in the twentieth century as a later book in the Old Testament saga, and by no means the least.

So much for man's history. My own was well into that phase euphemistically called "middle-aged"—a friend of mine says, "How many people over a hundred do *you* know?"—when all youthful hopes for one's family and career are in some disarray of shreds. This

was the thematic well for the play, and it was more than deep enough; in a hundred pages of dialogue I could hope only to dip into it, but it was my warrant to write a play personal to me. Its theme would be that of the dream aspired to, the price paid, and the reality we settle for.

The difficulty was of course structural; for weeks I'd been casting about in conventional terms for an adversary—I am acquainted with the practices of conventional drama—and gradually put away such preconceptions; the moment I began writing, I moved by intuition into a nonlinear design.

Its premise was that of a recognizable portrait, with background figures. I postulated that if that portrait were human enough, rich with trouble and the lady's own humor, it would hold the stage; and she would serve as a kind of tour guide through the country I wished to cross. The play announced itself at the outset as nonrepresentational. Its primary level was given by actors numbered, not named, who moved furniture and props in and out, paused in these chores to speak as "witnesses" of episodes remote in time and place from the main action, and unconcealedly assumed a succession of identities as the need arose; they were functionaries, not characters. The spinal action, the Yom Kippur War, a disaster which called into question the lady's life and its values, constituted the second level. This much was "realistic"; her decisions in the war, chronicled in succinct but precise detail, were written as consecutive drama. The third level was that of memory, a summoning-up of turning-points in her past—some schematic, some in full scenework—which, like the wit-

nesses, were inconsecutive but associatively related to the events of the war.

The war I hoped would be the line of suspense which held all taut; the interweaving of the presentational, realistic, and memory levels would make for a multi-angled look at not only the lady, but the history she had helped create; the drama was to be as much public as personal. It was the public scale of the content which pushed the play into its multiple form.

It did more; my head was full of the documentation I'd been digging into, and I ordained as the setting a backdrop on which to project a stream of "visuals"—films, stills, maps, dates, locales—intended to widen the play's horizons into history proper. This brilliant vision, which seduced everyone on the production crew, would prove in practice to be about the worst idea I ever had.

Little of the structure was formulated in my thoughts as it is here; it was felt, and emerged as I wrote, improvisatorily, sitting to it pretty much around the clock for the next two and a half months, the pages tumbling out of me. In January I typed them all up, and stepped out of the dream.

4.

My first chore in the outer world was to find a director and an actress. The noon I finished typing I gave a copy to my friend Arthur Penn, and we met the next morning; he said yes, he would direct, and within the hour I took off for Israel. In my absence he was to

invite Anne Bancroft to play Golda. It was almost aca-
demic; she had sent me press reports of her approval of
the script, which refuted others announcing the production was off because she hated the first act and
should be ashamed of herself after all I'd done for her;
the pages in question were not yet out of my type-
writer. Already we were more news-event than art.

My second chore was to get the real Golda's approval.
By contract she had the right to veto only an outline
of the play; I had no outline, but came up with one
ex post facto, and at Langner's request bore it to her
in person. I was not unabashed about the mission—this
woman had negotiated implacably with the potentates
of the world—but all it took was time.

In Lou's apartment I talked my way through the
outline, and a noncommittal Golda asked me to repeat
my performance for her family. I did, in the Ramat
Aviv home for her sister, son, daughter-in-law, and
grandson, and in the Negev kibbutz for her daughter,
son-in-law, and granddaughter; meanwhile, copies were
in the mail to the two women who were her literary
helpers, Rinna Samuel in Rehovot and Marie Syrkin in
California. This procedure ate up most of February.
I reminded Golda that Langner was waiting for a green
light to raise money, and she nodded, but would offer
no hint until all the votes were in; and I went off hiking
for a week in the Mt. Sinai range. The day the California approval came she said yes, and I cabled Langner.

I then said I was prepared to read the play itself to
Golda, but alone. I was given three hours in a room in
the King David Hotel, and had to pass into it through
both Israeli and American security; our secretary-of-

state, Cyrus Vance, had taken over a floor—we were in Israel simultaneously three times and I thought it uneconomical, one of us could have also done the other's business—and was scheduled to see Golda at five o'clock.

I began reading at two-thirty. I had stipulated we be alone because there were political and personal items in the script I suspected Golda didn't know I knew; I anticipated also a kind of crosseyed shock in her at hearing dialogue so fictional about matters so factual. Time in mind, I asked that we not discuss details, if she grunted whenever she objected I would check the margin for argument later. She grunted three times in the first ten pages, and thereafter fell silent, smoking her cigarettes; once she asked, "Who says that?" and I said, "You," an instant which contained this entire historical oddity; and I read on to the halfway break.

I said, "Is it hard to take?"

She said, "It's overwhelming, I'm listening like it's somebody else."

At four minutes to five I said, looking up, "I have three pages to go, I think I can finish."

She waved her hand, "Go on, go on."

I closed the script at one minute to five, stood up, and bummed one of her cigarettes; she rose and opened the balcony door-windows, clearing the room of her smoke for Vance.

She said, "What you've done is great, if people can follow it they'll go crazy. You have to take out about—"

And she named the one item I expected.

I said, "We'll talk," and left fast.

And that was almost that. Lou conveyed to me a

request that I stay in Israel three more weeks until Golda's son returned from Europe to hear the play; while waiting I met with Golda again in her office near her home, went over some questions I had, and discussed the item. It was personal, had never been in print, and I began to explain my deductive cleverness.

Golda said, "I didn't ask you how you found out."

I said, "Did I hurt you when I read it?"

She said simply, "Yes."

I was moved by that moment, and didn't argue the point, I felt she had a moral if not contractual right to excise it. I blacked it out before I read the play again in Israel. Twice was to my own friends, who thought it "wonderful," it would "run for three years"; the last reading was in Golda's home to some fifteen people—her relatives, lawyer, lady doctor, literary advisor Rinna, others, and Lou—who were critical only of scattered details, and when I phoned Lou the next day she said, "I think they were stunned."

This seemed a good note on which to come home, and I did.

5.

The trouble with playwriting is that the act of writing, which for me is the cream, is only the top of the bottle. A poem or book when written is done with; a play is a kind of notation until produced, and the writer accompanies it on one of the most treacherous expeditions known to man, show business. I have not one

friend in it who hasn't donated huge sums to therapists to help stave off insanity, with inconspicuous success.

Penn I found rational enough, at work on the set and visuals; he had come to Israel for two weeks to look into war films, and now he, the set and light designers, the crew collating the materials, were all excited by the chance to do something "revolutionary, a breakthrough" in mixed-media staging. Bancroft flew in from Hollywood to go over the script with us, told her husband there was "no way I'm not going to do it," and in June took off for Israel with my wife to spend ten days at Golda's elbow, soaking her up. We felt in luck to land an actor and an actress we liked for Golda's husband and Lou; the other casting was casual, we read nobody, actors came into Penn's office whom he knew, chatted with us, and were hired.

The set moved off Santo Loquasto's drawing-sheets to materialize as a model, and was a black beauty. A most ingenious solution for the projections, its raison d'être, it consisted—apart from a raked stage with two small platforms, all carpeted black—of a scrim angling up from the rear to the front; overhead, between scrim and backwall, was hung a stagewide bank of mirrors, to double the throw; and in the flies were some thirty projectors, a few for films, the others for slides, which would bounce images off the mirrors onto both the backwall and the see-through scrim's backside. This shifting counterpoint of multiple visuals on each of two planes was to be supplemented by a pair of television cameras above the two platforms onstage; when actors fingered military maps, the maps and fingers would appear in live magnification on two screens

moving in and out, and all details of the war be clear.

A cartographer designed us the maps, very handsome and expensive; the film crew was cutting up the reels air-freighted to us by the Israeli state bureau and a film-maker on salary in Jerusalem; the slides crew was nose-deep in stills culled from museums, old newspapers, and a photographer on salary in Tel Aviv; and in July I flew to Israel a third time, to ferret out items still lacking.

I returned in August, when we went into rehearsal to a hoopla of press attention the like of which none of us had ever seen. A photo of Bancroft with Golda had appeared throughout the world, and in New York on a front page; and the first hours of rehearsal were overrun by a score of reporters and photographers, from the city dailies, magazines, out-of-town newspapers; a TV network crew set up shop in an adjoining room to catch all of us for interviews. It was the noisiest sendoff in theatre annals, good only for ticket sales. I was uneasy, we still had to deliver a show, and I said to Penn this was a fat turkey to cut into, I could hear the critics sharpening their knives.

But rehearsals were smooth; in the bare studio, with a couple of boxes for a set, the pieces of the play fell naturally into place.

Our expectations ran high. The actors were enthusiastic, as always, and more than one told me how they'd wept over the script. I had read it twice to friends at home, once to a group of writers and their wives, half of them Jewish, once to a group of Catholics with whom I'd been staging my church plays; in both groups the pitch of ecumenical fervor swept listeners

off to Langner to invest in the show, against my advice. The budget was astonishing, half a million dollars. But the money had come in swiftly, and advance sales were excellent; it seemed we had no problems.

Penn had attended my second reading, and afterwards I'd observed it certainly looked like an audience show; but he was most thoughtful about the projections, said they were not easy.

I said, "Do you think we could do it without?"

He said, "It could live that way."

It was our total look into that possibility, and later I would kick myself for not pursuing it.

The third day into rehearsal I whispered to him my doubts about certain actors; he agreed, but time was ample, he was confident they would work out. Bancroft was feeling her way slowly, but I had no concern about her, she was solid. And what I was most obtuse to was a process so insidious that not until months later, in editing the text for publication, did my eyes open to it: we were all being seduced away from the play's true nature by our own, our inheritance as workers in the American theatre, a turn of mind toward realism.

I repeat, the structure was known to me only intuitively; Penn and I never discussed it, both believing we understood it, and each assuming the other knew what he was doing; but I had simply not thought it through. We therefore had no concept of staging expressive of it. In the first minute of playing, Golda getting out of bed in a nightgown discards it to walk in a dress across the stage and into a group—identified only as "1st, 2nd, 3rd actors"—who are putting together her desk and

office; the opening image was antirealism. In rehearsal Penn sent her momentarily offstage to change in some unseen bathroom, a realistic touch, and the set was designed as a perfect entity in itself, nothing addable or subtractable, the numbered actors entered a preexistent office. That the stylistic premise of the text was thus negated, neither of us noticed, and every choice we made was equally against its grain. Bancroft in make-up was so startling in her likeness to Golda that Penn and I were delighted, and blind to its implications. In her seventies the character remembers herself at seventeen, being courted; these pages were written to be played with the two actors seated in separate pools of light, facing front. Our actors, steeped in Stanislavskian realism, ached to play them "with truth" in face-to-face confrontations, and I said fine; in performance thus we had an aged Golda, in false nose, jowl wattles, thick body-stocking, swollen leg, skipping around the stage as an adolescent girl, a grotesque sight disruptive of all truth and illusion. Which in the theatre are one. Langner came to me to say the audience ought to know who the numbered actors were, couldn't we list them in the program as Dayan, Bar-Lev, and so on?—and I said certainly, colluding in setting up the audience's expectations of dimensional characters the writing was never intended to fulfil. Our instinct for realism was warping the entire production, and none of us knew it.

All this was hidden from our eyes when, after three weeks of rehearsal, we gave two run-throughs before leaving for Baltimore. In a small theatre, to a couple of hundred people, the actors performed the script as a bare-stage presentation, no lights, no sound, no cos-

tumes, no make-up, no set, no visuals. The audience supplied it all in imagination—one said of the opening, "Anne Bancroft lay down and Golda got up"—and it played effortlessly; people laughed, cried, and congratulated us afterwards.

In good spirits I drove that night to Baltimore: I knew of a serene state park twenty minutes from downtown, looked forward with pleasure to a tent in the living woods instead of a dead hotel, and even thought my presence would be unnecessary after a couple of days.

6.

In Baltimore the roof fell in. I speak figuratively, although a comparable calamity was to befall us literally, in Boston; by then it was but one of our troubles.

The reviews were the worst in my life. Whether it was the text itself, or the lack of a staging concept to deliver it, or the deluge of theatre arts which now swamped it, its shifting structure was seen by our first-nighters as only a mish-mash; their coughings made more noise than the war. Some reviewers wrote like nincompoops—one said he expected a musical and it should have been, another in his first paragraph denounced our "million-dollar" advance—but the unblinkable fact was that we hadn't pleased any; all thought it a long-winded, confused, aimless bore, and in unanimously lauding Bancroft said she "got no help from the script."

Bancroft said, "They think I make up those lines out there."

Penn was calm, said, "It won't take much to turn that around."

But the reviews would have justified Langner in closing the show, and Penn and I faced a not unusual choice, watch it die or rewrite to make it work. I spent a day and a half digesting all that newsprint, which didn't swallow easily, and two nights studying the audience; then I sat backstage with Penn under a battery of light-handles.

I said, "Arthur, I think we'd better make this as much a linear play as we can."

I still did not understand what I had written.

Penn said, "I think so."

And thereafter for six weeks we worked in a close joy of collaboration, extremely hard, extremely well, and extremely in the wrong direction; other mistakes were made, mine was seminal.

The daily routine was enlivening. I'd sleep deliciously in the woods, make breakfast on a small fire, and until noon sit on a pad under an oak, deleting and rewriting; in the theatre all afternoon I'd watch Penn rehearse the actors in the cuts and new pages; and that same evening we'd have the changes in front of an audience to see how they worked. It was an exhilarating procedure, for us. It was a frantic one for the actors, never a rehearsal without great chunks to be unlearned and learned, and one said they were taking to hiding whenever they saw Penn or me. The Langners—Philip, his wife Marilyn, his mother Armina Marshall—came back on the weekend and were much gratified; in a week

we'd cut twenty minutes out of the first act and had the audience's attention, plus their tears and cheers at the close. Good word-of-mouth so overcame the bad reviews that in our third week, without subscription, we equalled the ticket sales of each of the first two, with. Agents and such theatre folk returned to check and said how stirred they were, the work was "wonderful," we had no worries; they were sincere, they meant it was moving closer to the kind of conventional play they were familiar with.

But I was trying to solve in the writing other problems which were not textual; it's the playwright's vanity to think nothing is his fault or everything.

The magic world of the theatre—our visuals, wigs, lighting, black set, costumes, sound effects, beards, vast house, inaudible actors and audible critics—had been dumped on the play overnight, and buried it. We spent much of our six weeks digging out from under the visuals alone, although anything that buried some of our actors I was in favor of. Friends inquired whether they were "really professionals," and the office staff never ceased to marvel at how we'd fished out "the worst actors in New York," so whether scenes I was deleting had sagged because of writing or acting was a tangled question. Penn was loth to fire any, kept hoping for rehearsal-time with them on old material, and made only one cast-change late in Boston at my insistence; I suggested three, wanted five. These generals forgot their lines when fingering maps—two couldn't read highway maps, one couldn't drive a car—and the television cameras projected every map as a smear, incorrigibly out-of-focus; the maps themselves were too

delicate to speak out, and I spent some hours in the basement with a stagehand pasting blue and red cut-outs of cardboard with blatant lettering over all the costly cartography, as in kindergarten; finally we threw out the cameras and the maps altogether. A later New York reviewer advised us we should have used maps. The stream of other visuals was so lethal to the dialogue of the military scenes—that body of fascinating material which interested no one, Bancroft said whenever the house started coughing she knew someone was behind her in uniform—that I cut the war to the merest mention possible. And this was the line I was hanging the play on. All computerized, the visual materials cost us I heard a hundred thousand dollars, and we jettisoned four-fifths of them; the rest we couldn't, it would have left us with a set consisting of a blank screen. And of two platforms, so functional that my "witnesses"—with no furniture or props now to move—had no business onstage, had lost their habitat, and entered only to orate; they had become a parade of intruders. Did I have the wit to see this as a directorial or design problem?—no, in the headlong course of production the quickest answer on any day is to knife out the question, and one after another I wrote the witnesses out of the play. And with them went what little of the presentational level we had tried for.

The finances of all this were outside my ken, I had my own problems, but whenever I wandered backstage I felt I was at the opera. Downstairs was a cell I invaded only once, a seeming chaos of our innumerable what, computers? and cables snaking everywhere, I suppose up to the projectors onstage; my ignorance made me

suicidal. Offstage was a room as big as a basketball
court hung with rank after rank of jackets, uniforms,
robes, and among them lived a people whose names
I never learned, dressers wished on us by their union;
here too, laid out along a mirrored table, was an
exhumatory display of severed beards and wigs on skulls,
tended by two lovely ghouls. Apart from stage crews,
doubled by our technology, we had close to thirty actors
and understudies. By some Equity foul-up, understudies
were earning more offstage than actors onstage, who
were in an unending dash to and from the wardrobe
room; all were doubling parts, doffing and donning
uniforms and beards, and running back in items whose
provenance remained a mystery to the end.

During one performance Penn said to me, "Do you
like Lou's wig?"

"No," I said, "why did you order it?"

He said, "I thought you ordered it."

So we both ordered it off her head. When the Israeli
ambassador to Washington, Dinitz, saw the actor who
functioned as him he said "not in his whole life" had
he owned so many suits. I dropped a minute out of the
show by cutting one witness, and two walk-ons—Arab
servants who in the dark laid a rug for the Abdullah
scene, and in the dark following it shot him—came to
tell us they couldn't make their change; we said, after
a month of playing, what change? and learned they
were each peeling off one Arab outfit and struggling
into another, both invisible; I examined the costumes
afterwards, four robes fit for a king.

Theatre money is stage-money; when I lamented

such waste, our business-manager said, "Don't take it personally."

The ambassador's visit opened a little adventure for Penn and me. Since Dinitz had first read the script the government of Israel had changed hands, he was now working for Dayan, and said I didn't do him justice. Lacking an interview, I had based his war positions on a book written by the Israeli ambassador to the UN, whom I did interview, as well as on other generals; and to Golda I'd said I hoped Dayan—who by then had deserted her party to join the new cabinet—would find what I'd written not inaccurate.

Golda said, "Let him write his own play."

Dinitz now suggested the book was in error, phoned New York, and two mornings later Penn and I were in a hotel suite there, ringed by Dayan in his eye-patch and three of his aides. After the war he'd been much hated and in eclipse for three years—"a man who has lost his world," said one journalist—and on my first visit was launching a tabloid which I believe folded; now he was back in power. He opened by saying how much he "loved Golda," and denied having refused to see me. I named his secretary, said I'd spoken to her four times, and quoted her message verbatim.

"I don't understand," said Dayan, "she's usually very truthful."

I refrained from saying so was I, but listened a bit skeptically thereafter. Dayan said I should have worked from *his* autobiography—he referred to it as "the book," his three aides all had copies in their laps—and I said I didn't see why I was to have taken his at face value

in preference to others, but would be happy to rewrite positions of his that at one point he called "a lie!" That eruption aside, he was affable, quick, rather unkempt and harried, answered everything by consulting "the book" with his aides, and after an hour turned me over to them.

I had no way of knowing what was truth; the play was in the crossfire of "the war of the generals"— an Israeli phrase designating those quarrels which had resulted in the postwar Agranat report exculpating the cabinet at the expense of the military, who therefore detested Dayan—and for my purposes one version was as good as another. Penn went about other business, and I sat all afternoon in a bedroom with the aides. Our task was to conflate patches of my dialogue and "the book," the ossified word which now stood in place of living memory; but then I saw it was Dayan's defense of his war-conduct for history, his rebuttal of the "lies" so current in Israel. I said if his book was true he must feel like a man who'd been crucified.

"That's how he feels," said an aide.

Late in the day Dayan came in from a nap to sit on the bed for my remaining questions. Among others, I asked could I relocate a colorful phrase of his by two days; he said absolutely not. I said I wanted to move Golda with it.

He said, "You move her with *your* words."

I thought this just enough. Dayan then commented favorably on my lack of a necktie and left me, and I left his aides. I rejoined Penn on the evening train for Baltimore.

The rest of the week I spent rewriting all the dialogue in question.

I had cabled Golda that our reviews were "worse than your October 6th," the disastrous first day of her war, but that we had time and were working hard. Now we moved out of town with a show in working order, confident that, eyeing our audiences, we had won the battle of Baltimore.

7.

Not so. Our move to Boston was so tight we had no time onstage before our preview, gave a weak and inaudible performance, and tried to postpone the critics on the following day, in vain; we performed much better for them, won a standing ovation, and the two big reviews were bad. Written by men friendly to me, one said the show was incomplete, the other called it "a platform harangue," and both—a new note—assailed Bancroft's work as mannered and unconvincing. It was vexing to be waylaid in the theatre alley by strangers with tears on their cheeks, thanking me for an experience no reviewer shared; none of my plays hitherto had elicited such a disparity.

Next day I drove in from my tent in another state park, and walked into the lobby to find Langner waiting; he said this show was "just like the S.S. *Pocahontas* trip"—see the play's first witness—and I said yes, but blankly enough that he said oh, then I didn't know

yet about the fire. Inside, the stage was a shambles of hanging shreds and swamplike carpeting, all the seats were doused and sooted, and below stage, among our dripping costumes and computers, water was a foot deep. Some cleaningwomen that morning had thrown a switch on a high-intensity quartz lamp next to a tormentor, and set us aflame; fire hoses did the rest.

Burned out, we were to play that night on a bare stage across the street. Penn had moved very fast; fearful that the lost income would close us for good, he'd phoned the Schuberts in New York, gotten use of their empty theatre, and was now setting up a dozen lights on its stage. That afternoon, back to the rehearsal boxes, our actors walked the play through, while in laundromats around town others of our crew were frantically drying out their costumes.

With its poverty-stricken look the evening performance was not unlike our two early run-throughs, and in the intermission Langner got me by the elbow.

"Did you hear?—they're absolutely with it, not a cough out of anyone."

It was true, all the visual adornments of the stage were subtractive. Penn said Loquasto, very gloomy, wanted to rethink his set, he felt it served the play poorly; I told Langner, and took off for home. I was now done with cutting, but had a scene to add we all agreed on, and one of the brighter actors had been pestering me for unwritten chunks not involving him but necessary to the theme; and the next two weekends at home I again wrote around the clock, material I felt and enjoyed. I pleased the actor, who said, "Now you've finished the play," but returning from the first weekend

I found the rethinking had issued—for sufficient reasons, no time, no money—in rebuilding the same set.

By midweek we were back on it, in our proper theatre. We played out our Boston run without further event—to full houses and standing ovations, the word-of-mouth was again at odds with the reviews—except for one ominous development: on Thursday Bancroft decided not to do a Saturday night show. She was weary, and the body-stocking was causing symptoms she offered to tell in private to any actor who asked.

I said, "Is it tell, or show and tell?"

She said, "It's tell."

She could not be dissuaded; we gave the performance, with her understudy, but refunded most of the box office to departing customers. In itself, the loss was absorbable, but. No longer writing, I grew inquisitive about our finances, and was flabbergasted to learn our break-even point was $93,000 a week; less in tickets and we couldn't pay our bills. And I knew Bancroft's frailties, her family had an Italian idiom for her that meant the one something's always wrong with.

Just before leaving Boston we asked one critic to come again and talk with us after. We had changed the show, but not his opinion of it; he offered two modest suggestions on script, felt the show didn't hang together, and still disbelieved its star performer. That I had taken out the last of the witnesses he thought "helpful."

Helpful, alas, he had no way of seeing—nor I yet—that it meant the total amputation of my primary level, the matrix of all the rest; we were coming in with two thirds of a play. It now announced itself as a wispily

realistic work with flashbacks, lacking a suspenseful line, adversaries, other characters of substance, one I would never have written by intent, and so simple-minded that I told my wife it would not see print; I would publish the original. Considering how I'd mutilated it, there was a lot of life in the old girl yet.

So we moved on, to New York and Golda.

8.

One aspect of this production I have not touched on, because I am unable to judge it.

This was a play about a woman much respected—Kissinger said that in all their dealings she "never did a second-rate thing"—but hardly uncontroversial, and a state no longer at the height of its fashion. The plight of the "third world," grown visible here via the magnifying lens of our black movement, had taken its place in liberal sympathies. When more than a year before I had listened to Golda speak at Wellesley, in return for an honorary degree, she was picketed by black and other radical students; in her dressing room Bancroft was opening fan mail that assailed her for portraying "an old war-hawk"; even my nephew's wife, a campus bride in the backwoods of Indiana, had said casually, "Of course, the way you feel about Jews, we feel about Arabs."

Doubtless these fissures ran through our audiences too, accounting for some dead spots, and live ones that

took me by surprise. Our most fervid enthusiasts were gentiles—one told me that at the end she "didn't feel like clapping, but praying"—and Jewish friends who were active in behalf of the Palestinian exiles avoided me. I also received some anonymous hate-mail, one sample suggesting that "the only way to alert the world to the dilemna [sic] of the jew is to keep producing these spectacles that make christians vomit. . . . you could start an air-sick bag business and have the consesion [sic] at all performances. . . . ve luv yu." From Boston, where John Cotton was spinning in his grave.

The play was not a neutral idyll; this is only a footnote.

9.

In New York the roof fell in, we were burned alive, bled on the cross of our own errors, and survived it all; it was a microbe that did us in.

But first came Golda. Undeterred by my cables— on the phone she told my wife, "Bill wrote such a beautiful play, it's a shame he has to have such aggravation"—she flew in as we were setting up for previews. She had in tow a party of relatives and friends she'd promised to bring from Israel for the opening, and my wife and I visited with them in her suite. It was not of course solely a personal trip. Golda is a state-furthering mammal as others are fur-bearing, and on our second night was the evening-gowned star at an Israel

Bonds dinner in the ballroom of her hotel. Planned months before around the show, it yielded in a kind of auction-bidding some six million dollars for the cause. That accomplished, Golda and everybody at the damasked tables took off for the theatre; the tickets came with the six million dollars.

It was a dim audience to pose the play's question for—Morris's on the state, "Goldie, Goldie, what went wrong?"—and Golda herself sat like marble throughout, petrifying the entire house around her. In the first minutes a paper in Bancroft's hands began shaking; later when I asked an actor how it felt he said fine till he'd looked into Bancroft's eyes, I asked what did he see, and he said, "Terror." Our best jokes dropped like boulders in the silence. The audience broke into one maniacal burst of applause when Ben-Gurion said "a Jewish woman got the money that made the state possible"; it was the only moment we gave them.

I was backstage when Golda trudged past in the narrow hall to Bancroft's dressing-room; I said, "Golda: surviving?" and not stopping she acknowledged me with a weak flip of her hand. After five minutes I went in to join them. They were seated together, in silence, at Bancroft's make-up table; and opposite, six feet away, sat Dinitz and his wife together, in silence. In the six feet between lay an invisible corpse.

I said, "Are you girls talking confidentially?"

Bancroft said, "She won't talk confidentially."

Golda remained silent, and after a wait I turned to Dinitz.

He whispered, out of respect for the corpse, "It's improved since Baltimore."

His wife whispered, "There's a *revolutionary* improvement since Baltimore."

I whispered, "Thanks," and fled.

This was Thursday night, and upon leaving Golda made an appointment with Penn for all of us to talk in her suite the next afternoon; I demurred, it was precious rehearsal-time, and Penn negotiated a change to Saturday morning at eleven.

There Golda sat behind a desk, and ranged around her, for Israel, were her son Menachem and daughter Sara, Lou, the literary advisors Rinna and Marie, and, for the show, Penn, Langner and his wife, I and mine. Bancroft was late. Rinna had flown in separately; over Europe the compression in her plane had failed, the oxygen masks dropped like oranges in a tree, the plane dove instantly from thirty thousand feet to five, and Rinna gave herself up to death; they landed somewhere, she phoned New York, arrived a day late, and Golda's first words to her were, "You think *you've* been in an accident?" The cross-eyed shock I had looked for, reading the play to her in Israel, had come.

Golda sent an emissary downstairs to head off Bancroft at the elevators, to spare her feelings. She had to say frankly the show was false and she detested everything in Bancroft's characterization; it was too old, feeble, stooped, limping, tearful, and shuffly with hands in pockets. And too yiddishe-momma, hadn't Marie written me she didn't use inversions? I quoted some from life—Sara whispered to my wife, "Does she?"—and Langner spoke eloquently for the defense, reading aloud an ecstatic fan-letter as evidence; but Golda was firm, said if she'd looked and sounded like Bancroft

she "could never have been elected prime minister."
Bancroft now walked in.

Golda said promptly, "That's it."

Bancroft said, astonished, "That's it? I missed everything?"

It was impossible that either of these two women
be spared, who at first meeting had fallen in love.
When I'd visited Israel later, Golda, speaking of a
garden party she had given for Bancroft and more
than a hundred guests, said there "wasn't one who
didn't love her," and I'd said, "Golda, she's an actress,
it's her business to make people love her," and Golda
said, "Even so, there's something so natural in her—"
And at their leavetaking Bancroft had said, "The next
time I see you, I'll be you!" If I'd written the script
in part as my gift to Golda, Bancroft was playing it as
hers; and Golda now had to say she rejected it.

And she did. Pulling no punches, she repeated her
indictment, in so level a voice it lacked personal affront;
and Bancroft listened in quiet, not a flicker of defensive-
ness, until Golda was finished.

She then moved her chair up to the desk, and said,
"Now you have to be specific. On what line do I put
my hands in my pockets?"

I listened to them talk it through, the better part of
an hour; it was a remarkable human exchange, and
afterwards I said so to Golda, and told Bancroft I was
proud she was my friend.

"Well," she said, shrugging, "what else could I do?"

I said, "You could have been a dumb blonde."

Bancroft went directly from that riddling to the

theatre to get into make-up, and played the matinee; grit personified, she gave a quite different performance, younger, strong, dry, simpler but valid. It was how she would act it thereafter. Rinna came to see it, noted the habitual ovation, told me the show was very effective, and reported back it was "not what she'd been led to believe."

Our opening had been deferred. Langner turned it instead into a "Golda Gala," with TV cameras in the street aiming at the limousine arrivals—the governor, the mayor, U.S. senators, movie stars, a houseful of other celebrities—and Golda again, with bodyguards. Present on compulsion, she must have dreaded the ordeal; certainly Bancroft did. But it was a good show, very up, and the audience was alive to every moment of it. And at its end, when the house stood clapping, Golda sat in tears.

Once more she trudged backstage, this time spreading joy to all, on her progress to Bancroft's dressing room.

She said, "I don't know how you did it in twenty-four hours."

Bancroft said, "I had forty-eight."

She'd had one. But she felt a bad let-down afterwards; depressed all the next week, she said "her performance had been taken away" and with it her confidence; and she didn't quite believe it was the happy ending it seemed. The real daughter Sara perhaps put into one word the sentiments of the Israelis when, asked if the show was not better, she said succinctly, "Somewhat."

Bancroft never altogether recovered her spirits, and after the reviews was a waiting prey for the microbe.

10.

The major reviews—excepting one rave on television, and a couple of others in minor publications—were dismal. I didn't see them all, because two days after we opened I was on a plane for Jerusalem, where I had an appointment with myself.

The night before, my wife and I called on Golda in her suite, and asked how she viewed Sadat's coming visit to the Knesset; the newspapers were hectic with it. Golda shook her head, said glumly he would "come and make a beautiful impression and leave us looking bad, it's very dangerous for us." I thought it party jealousy, but again she had simply gone to the heart of it; all she said came true.

I was in an Arab eatery in the Old City the night Sadat's plane landed; there were five tables, with a portable TV on one showing the arrival, and the dozen customers—Arabs, Israelis, foreigners—brought their plates to it, sitting together in excited good will. The joy on both sides of the city was high, peace on everyone's tongue, and families ran into King David Street to have their photos taken under the lightpoles hung alternately with Israeli and Egyptian flags; even my young apolitical friends were "thrilled." The peoples of the world are one thing, their leaders not quite another, and therein lies the dybbuk.

I did some hiking and other things, for a month, but mostly sat in the sun on the same rooftop overlooking the walled city, editing the script for publication. It was zestless. I kept regurgitating the production every day, trying to understand my part in all that had intervened between script and opening; and at last I saw it.

There was an obvious hypothesis: the script was boring, had always been boring, and would always be boring, however staged. But this ignored the early data. To people who read it, or heard me read it, the script was a transparency; imagining Golda and everything in it, they saw and believed the reality behind it. All literature, fictions too, refers to a reality behind it; we call it truth to life, or we disbelieve. The reality here was history. In production we had substituted for typescript a stage imitation of history which was not itself believable—one critic, a friend, called it "absurd"— and, in addition, occluded the reality behind it. What was necessary was staging that made no bid as realism, a style of artifice, which would be as transparent as the typescript. But this was exactly what I had written into it as its presentational level, and, in a derring-do of self-surgery no one asked for, had knifed out.

I refrained from jumping off the rooftop; instead, I phoned Langner—who was more concerned to tell me of Bancroft's demand that we drop one performance a week—and said I'd like a meeting three mornings later. I flew home, and in his office made my pitch to him, Armina Marshall, their business manager, Penn, and my wife. The advance sales guaranteed us months of playing time; I said we should take advantage of it to get rid of the remaining visuals, use the scrim to seat

all the actors behind in dim light, restage the text I'd brought back in a style supportive of it, and invite the critics to review us again. Langner was willing, but his business manager was dubious, and Penn said it would be a makeshift undertaking inside the old shell. And Bancroft was exhausted, couldn't play the present schedule, let alone rehearse also.

When I went backstage she was wan, demoralized, miserable, weeping nightly in the play when Morris said to her, "Goldie, Goldie, what went wrong?" Trapped in a six-month contract, she ached to be home in California. And the performance I caught was so pale, in all the actors, I found it painful; the stage manager told me it was "high by comparison," Bancroft was jacking herself up for me.

I went to my home, luckier, and by hearsay in the next month was kept apprised of a running sore between her and the office. She was cancelling a performance each week for reasons they and the actors thought wilful—a sore toe, her child's cold—and those of us on royalties waived them to keep the show above its break-even point. Theatre parties were phoning in frantic, would they see Bancroft or not, and current sales fell off by half. The one day I drove down she was out; I hung around the lobby, jammed with people turning back tickets, and overheard a man complain it was his second time. Langner quoted someone who had come three times, futilely.

I was not astonished when, soon after, the microbe invaded that thin body; she was undeniably sick, a strep throat, and for fifteen days the theatre was dark. The owners exercised their stop-clause and sent us a

two-week notice of eviction, they would bring in a reliable musical. Langner offered to stay dark. Bancroft said no, she wanted to "finish the show on my feet"; she came back to overflow houses for the last ten performances, played five, and collapsed.

So this little candle on the menorah guttered out.

*   *   *

Early in the project someone said, "Langner has lucked into something so good here—"

By which was meant Bancroft, Penn, and me: a unique actress whose illnesses cost the production half a million in lost income, a fine director almost totally ignored in reviews which needed every inch to list the play's faults, and a writer too slow-witted to follow the workings of his own pencil. For such luck I can only apologize.

Here then is the script which survives; begun in Jerusalem, finished in Jerusalem, much operated on in between, it is now restored with all its limbs and flourishes. I hope it flourishes, I'm fond of it, it is the play I meant to write. It may not be a dead duck. But the bird of fable, that rose again when consumed in fire by its own act, was the only one in the world.

GOLDA

A PARTIAL PORTRAIT

Cast

1ST WITNESS   (*also Abdullah, Ben-Gurion, TV inter-*
                 viewer, Religious Minister, DP)

GOLDA

1ST ACTOR   (*also Morris, 5th Witness, DP*)

2ND ACTOR   (*also TV assistant, 6th Witness, DP*)

3RD ACTOR   (*also Arab, father, 4th Witness, British*
                 commandant, DP, cabinet minister)

4TH ACTOR   (*also bodyguard, chairman, DP, 7th*
                 Witness, cabinet minister)

5TH ACTOR   (*also 2nd Witness, Arab, Menachem,*
                 DP, cabinet minister)

LOU   (*also Clara middle-aged, DP*)

SMALL GIRL   (*also Sarile as child, DP*)

SISTER   (*also young girl, Clara teen-aged, Amer-*
                 ican girl, DP)

MOTHER   (*also 3rd Witness, Sarile middle-aged,*
                 DP)

BOY   (*also DP*)

YOUNGER BOY   (*also DP*)

The Set

Up left, a platform used as Golda's office, with a step or two down, but enterable from any side.

Down right, a low platform used as a bed, table, and otherwise; it leads to a higher platform, up right.

Deep rear, a row of chairs—brought from time to time onstage—on which the company sits betweenwhiles.

The Staging

The play must announce itself at the outset as nonrepresentational. Ninety-nine per cent factual, it is a documentary fantasia on a moral theme, and is structured on three levels, presentational, linear, and memory.

On the presentational level the numbered actors are functionaries, not dimensional characters, who create the settings, address the audience as story-tellers, and—except for Golda—assume a succession of identities as the need arises. The second level is conventionally linear, the "present time" of the Yom Kippur War of 1973. The third is memory, a summoning up in Golda of turning-points in her past which, like the "witnesses," are related associatively to the events of that war.

The movement, lighting, and other aspects of direction must establish these levels. Whatever means the actor uses to differentiate his roles—costume bits, hair, props, whatnot—his changes should be recognizable, an integral part of the staging concept. This artifice is the stage reality, a transparency, through which the historical reality may speak.

ACT I

THE COMPANY SEATS ITSELF AT REAR, HOUSELIGHTS STILL
ON.

THE 1ST WITNESS COMES DOWN, SPREADS A BLANKET ON
THE PLATFORM DOWN RIGHT, AND ADDRESSES US.

1ST WITNESS: Golda?—well, I'll tell you a fable. But true!
—everything here is true, and one plot.

In 1921 two dozen of us came over to Palestine
with her. Young, socialists, stars in our eyes. Nine
days it took us to sail from New York to Boston,
with a strike—and sabotage, one sailor yells at me,
Your ship'll sink in mid-ocean! And it takes us,
the two-week trip to Naples, forty-four days. The
crew is mixing seawater into our drinking water,
and the pumps and boilers start breaking down;
the captain puts one seaman in irons; then the
sailors leave portholes open and the food gets
ruined, and all the books her young husband
Morris brought are waterlogged. Golda meanwhile
is on deck studying Hebrew. Fire breaks out in
two bunkers, the engine room is flooded and the
ship leans sideways; the captain puts the dynamo
men in irons. At the Azores we stop for repairs,

they try to burn the ship. Four engineers are heard
saying they'll sink it before Naples, the captain
puts them in irons. And finally the captain com-
mits suicide by throwing himself overboard; when
they find his body somebody's tied his hands together to a pipe. So?—two dozen young idealists
sailing off to Utopia, and below-decks human
nature doing all it can to sink the ship.

The question is, did it?—that's the plot, stars in
your eyes, you reach! and end up holding, what,
one more match in the dark?

(*The house and stage go dark, a long moment.*)

(*Sound begins, whispers, lapping of water, a tramp-
ing of many feet; a shofar is blown, and dies away;
a plane streaks overhead, and is gone; distant bells
toll four o'clock.*)

(*A phone rings, down right, and presently a spot-
light steals on;* GOLDA *elbowing up out of the blanket—seventy-five, in a nightwrap, hair in a braid,
heavy-voiced and slow—picks up the phone.*)

GOLDA: Yes, what? . . . Ah, no, no—I knew, yesterday,
in my bones. . . . No, look, I'll meet as soon as
Moshe and Dado talk, when? . . . Then seven.
Tell the others, my—

(*She hangs up, bitterly—*)

—generals—

(—*lights a cigarette, and gets out of bed, an aged
lioness, pinning up her hair.*)

—half my cabinet, generals—

(*Up left four actors come—two in open shirts,
Israeli style, two in army khaki—with chairs and a
desk, creating* GOLDA's *office in rising daylight on
the platform.*)

—and not one of them could smell yesterday under
his nose that today it's war?

(*Sound erupts, a vast rumbling of trucks, tanks
grinding, engines revving up, a clamor of foreign
voices—it breaks off, the actors motionless and
listening, a tableau; they recite chorus-like, and
only gradually move into realistic playing.*)

1ST ACTOR: The intelligence was shit. Yesterday—
2ND: Calmly.
3RD [KHAKI]: The intelligence was right, we read it
     wrong.
1ST: Who read it wrong?
2ND: Yesterday the United States read it wrong.
4TH [KHAKI]: Yesterday we gave her bad advice, all of us.
     If—
3RD: Yesterday I said the Russians leaving Damascus—
GOLDA [HEAVY]: Yesterday was yesterday, let's agree to

one thing, that word we don't hear again in this office.

(*Dropping the nightwrap behind, in a plain wash-dress she trudges to join them; they move in and out around her, bringing her papers—a woman,* LOU, *now among them.*)

Today we'll have time for one luxury only, to be attacked, when?

3RD: Six this evening.

GOLDA: So, we have ten hours. Look, I must talk to Dinitz and Keating.

(LOU *goes out;* GOLDA *presides at the desk, flanked by the* 1ST *and* 4TH *actors; the* 1ST *puts on an eye-patch.*)

On the call-up, the two of you agree?

1ST: Disagree, we've brought it to you.

GOLDA [PONDEROUS]: Thank you.

4TH: I want a full mobilization for counterattack.

1ST: I say mobilize what we need to hold the lines, that's our first job—

4TH: I want to break their bones and cross the Canal.

1ST: Counterattack can wait, Golda, Dado is too— enthusiastic. There's a political consideration too, if again the world calls us the aggressor—

GOLDA: Look, political reasons I don't need to hear, military I do.

4TH: Facts, not enthusiasm—

1ST: Mobilize for defense now—

4TH: —we know what the Syrians have, over nine hundred tanks, we have 177—

1ST: —and call up the rest tonight.

4TH: When they're across the Jordan?

GOLDA: *I* have to decide between our Minister of Defense and Chief of Staff?—

1ST: Dear Prime Minister—

GOLDA: —how does a woman decide between generals?

2ND [A DRAWLER]: It comes with the job.

GOLDA [PAUSE]: All right, the world calling us a bad name isn't such a new burden; but Syrian tanks in our backyard? I'm sorry, Moshe—

1ST: I don't insist.

GOLDA: —the call-up must be as Dado wants.

4TH: I also want a first strike.

1ST: No.

GOLDA: Preempt.

4TH: Hit them before they hit us, minutes count—

1ST: No. I do insist—we'll be condemned everywhere, get no help from anyone—

GOLDA [TO 4TH]: The Americans told Dinitz a hundred times don't preempt, Eban don't preempt, me don't preempt—

4TH: I can take out the Syrian airfields and missiles by noon if you move this minute.

GOLDA: You'll guarantee a six-day war again?

4TH: I guarantee you a thousand dead soldiers if you don't.

GOLDA: Dado, I have to guarantee three million live civilians. In a week we'll need help, and from the Americans; you'll risk that?

(A 5TH *actor comes to poke his head in;* LOU
follows.)

5TH: The Lady wants me.

GOLDA: Dinitz, come in.

4TH: It will save lives—

GOLDA [RISES]: More than help from the Americans?

2ND: If they help.

GOLDA: I guarantee that; Dinitz will see to it. It's not
here I want you, Simcha, it's ringing Kissinger's
doorbell.

5TH: I know—

GOLDA: How soon can you fly back?

5TH: Yom Kippur, nothing's moving—

GOLDA: You are.

LOU: The military will fly him to Cyprus; from there—

(*The desk phone rings, she answers it.*)

5TH: —but this evening, if I can—

GOLDA: It's too late.

5TH: Well, if I—

GOLDA: Now. The minute you see Kissinger, the first
point—

LOU: The American ambassador.

GOLDA [TAKES PHONE]: Mrs. Meir. . . . Not so good, our
neighbors are calling on us today. With Soviet
tanks. . . . We hear six o'clock. . . . Look, I have
one message for Washington—we can strike first,
and won't. . . . Can and won't, we promise won't,
it's maybe not too late if the President calls on
Moscow. . . . Yes, the Russians know, they all flew

home from Damascus yesterday—they supply the arms, their best friends the corpses. . . . Thank you.

(*She hangs up, walks the 5TH to the threshold.*)

Kissinger now, the first point is we did as they said about a first strike, the second is where are the forty-eight Phantoms.

5TH: I'll push, of course I'll push—

GOLDA: The third is resupply, Nixon promised we'd—

(*Sound explodes—artillery bombardment, the roar of tanks and planes, and the air-raid sirens of Israel begin to wail here and there, climbing to full-out; the lights change to night as the actors scatter, one setting up a mike at center; GOLDA comes heavily to it with a speech the 3RD gives her, puts on glasses, and begins to read.*)

GOLDA: Citizens of Israel. Ordeal by battle has been forced on us again.

Shortly before 2:00 P.M. today the armies of Egypt and Syria launched a series of attacks in Sinai and on the Golan Heights. The Israel Defense Forces have entered the fight—our sons.

We too must make any sacrifice for our independence, our freedom, our survival—

(*She breaks off, closes her eyes, covers the mike with a hand—*)

—our survival—

(—*as the lights change to "memory light," and*
GOLDA *goes deep into herself, speaking not to us:*)

Survival is maybe a synonym for Jewish. The first
thing I remember is my father, Moishe the car-
penter, nailing boards across a door in Kiev, to
keep out a pogrom. In those days pogroms were
—oh, the fashionable thing, hundreds, no town
without one—

(*Lights on the platform up right—dreamlike, Russia 1904—and a small girl dressing a doll; her older
sister watches her; their mother comes in with
a plate.*)

—with Jews everywhere mourning, fasting—
MOTHER: Goldie, you left your plate, now I want you
to eat—

(*The small girl ignores it, and the mother turns on
the sister.*)

She's fasting too?—
SMALL GIRL: I'm fasting too—
MOTHER: —a wonderful example you set her, every day
in black, why are you doing this to me?
SISTER: Momma, children are dead.
GOLDA [TO US]: —and I'm fasting—
SMALL GIRL: —for the children they killed.
MOTHER: So if you don't eat you'll be another; take a—
Gevalt, she's dressing the doll in black!

(*She jumps up, horrified.*)

Moishe, Moishe!—oh, this Goldie has a dybbuk in her—

(*She hurries out, the sister after; the small girl is left alone, in fading light, and sound steals in around her—hoofbeats, rising into shouts, windows smashing, a pogrom—then breaks off; the small girl stands screaming, screaming.*)

(*Lights out on her;* GOLDA *puts aside the mike, speaks to us.*)

GOLDA: I have a dybbuk, yes, over and over in me it says, Live. Live, did I make it up?—God said, I've set before you two things, life and death, therefore choose life. And the dybbuk says, Here is a dream, a new land, more life for all—more life for all—

(*She turns up to her office, pauses heavily.*)

—so send the young to die. It has two tongues, this dybbuk—more life, more death—

(*The* 3RD *actor comes to take the speech, and* GOLDA *mounts to her office;* LOU *brings in a tray of coffee, and* GOLDA *sits to the desk.*)

GOLDA: Lou, go home and sleep.
LOU: After you.

GOLDA: I'm sleeping here, on the couch, and for two there isn't room.

LOU: First, my dear lady, you will not sleep three winks here; and second, you cannot conduct this war properly without a fresh dress.

GOLDA [TO HERSELF]: Such very young boys out there, dying—

LOU: Sanctifying the name of God.

GOLDA: —I have no way to stop it. What?

LOU: It's one way the rabbis say a Jew can sanctify the name of God, to die defending other Jews.

GOLDA [PAUSE]: Bring me a dress, tomorrow.

(LOU *nods, leaves;* GOLDA *sits over coffee and ciga-rette, mulling. The* 2ND *Witness comes to take the mike; he is the* 5TH *actor, costumed for a different role.*)

2ND WITNESS: Golda, yes, my story is from early in '47, before the state, when our boys were ambushed by Arabs on their way to Etzion. She'd become the head of the Agency—the only one the British didn't lock up in Latrun—and I remember she made a statement, she said Jews had been dying long enough for no cause, it was time they died for their own. We were smuggling messages into the prison with the food, and Sharett read it there— she was taking his place—and sent word out it was true but "bitter as death." Well, after the ambush Golda insisted on going not only to the hospital, but into the morgue, alone. I watched, there were eight dead boys in a row on the floor, and Golda

just stood looking at them, for two minutes. If she
was religious I'd say she was praying; but it was
her way of saying, I am at one with you.

(*He takes the mike off, left; down right the* 3RD
and 4TH *actors spread a map on the low platform,*
and GOLDA *rises to come down to them.*)

GOLDA: Don't be kind to the old, Dado, how does it
　　　look?
4TH: The Golan is not good. The main thrust is devel-
　　　oping down here, Kudne, Rafid, Juhader, at least
　　　four hundred Syrian tanks here; the Barak Brigade
　　　is being chewed up from A6 to 10—
GOLDA: How many tanks in our Barak?
3RD: The Barak is down to twenty.
GOLDA: What?
4TH: Less.
GOLDA: It's nothing, how can it be less, where are the
　　　reserves we called up?
4TH: Just coming. The 79th is here on the Yehudia road
　　　now—
GOLDA: So it's a race.
4TH: For the Jordan. If they overrun headquarters at
　　　Nafekh there's nothing between them and us, and
　　　we'll blow the bridges.
GOLDA: Give me a cigarette. What's the airforce doing?
3RD: Bombing the Canal.
GOLDA: Look, the Canal is Africa, the Jordan is our
　　　back door; call them—
4TH: Moshe did, they'll be there with first light.
GOLDA: Another hour.

3RD: It won't be like '67, we're losing planes very fast—

GOLDA [UNBELIEVING]: To Egyptians?

3RD: To missiles, Soviet SAM's—

4TH: We're flying into the most concentrated surface-
to-air network we've—

GOLDA: They said they could take out the missiles, first
thing.

3RD: They can't give close support and take out the
missiles both.

4TH: I asked for a first strike.

GOLDA [PAUSE]: See if Dinitz got to Washington yet.

(*The* 3RD *picks up a phone; the* 4TH *starts out.*)

Dado. I'm learning here.

4TH: I know. That's all we have as of now, Golda—

3RD [HANGS UP]: I'll keep you in touch with the reports
coming in—

4TH: Shalom—

(*The two men withdraw.*)

GOLDA [HEAVILY]: Shalom, shalom.

(*She sits alone, with eyes closed, and goes into
herself; the lights change to memory.*)

Israel. Israel, born 1948; died—? A little each day
since, six thousand of us that first summer, one
out of ten—

(*The lights find* MORRIS, *silhouetted behind her;
he is the* 1ST *actor, minus the eyepatch.*)

MORRIS: It never stopped, did it? Such a dream, the
state, an irony—

GOLDA [NOT TURNING]: Morris—

MORRIS: —that this is the one place in the world where
Jews are in danger; all your life given for a state,
Goldie, next week you'll have it, and only here
could we be wiped out.

GOLDA: Morris, enough!—so jealous of what we all
dreamed—

MORRIS [MILDLY]: Goldie, you dreamed of a paradise,
what went wrong?

(GOLDA *sits morose, not looking at him; he turns
to leave, stops.*)

Are you happy, at last?

GOLDA: Happy I never thought of, every day something
impossible to do, who had time?

MORRIS: Oh, I had time.

GOLDA: You thought make a nice home, read a book,
be happy—

MORRIS: Such a dream.

GOLDA: —you should have married my mother. I thought
make a new world—

MORRIS: Whoever it cost.

GOLDA: —what else did we think of but work for it?
Fifteen hours a day in meetings and offices, and
three-thirty in the morning one man said, Goldie,
don't come in early tomorrow, come at eight.

MORRIS [SUDDENLY]: Which man, why did we come to
    this beggarly land!
GOLDA: It's ours.

(*The lights lose* MORRIS; GOLDA *sits alone, eyes
closed.*)

Such a dream, what went wrong?

(*She stands—twenty-five years younger, moves ac-
cordingly—and speaks to us:*)

All right, not a state yet, May 10th, 1948—

(*The* 2ND *actor enters in a khaffiyeh—as her escort,
a different role—and comes to her with a black
Arab robe.*)

—five days to statehood, with how many Arabs
    around us?—
2ND: Ninety million.
GOLDA [TO HIM]: —sworn to drive us into the sea; and
    at the last minute Ben-Gurion sends me begging for
    peace.
2ND [ROBES HER]: I'll wear this, and trust my Arabic.
    You will wear this, and be mute.
GOLDA: That will be the hardest.
2ND: Who else knows?
GOLDA: Here?—you and Ben-Gurion. There, I'm not
    so sure.
2ND: Oh, the King will be discreet, it's worth his life
    too.
GOLDA: Too?

2ND: The danger is real. If we're stopped, don't show
fear; no believer will touch a strange woman.

GOLDA: And if it's an infidel?

2ND: I convert him. We'll change cars several times
before Naharayim, to be sure we're not followed;
from there we'll be driven to a house in Amman—

(*Fixing her veil, he takes the cigarette out of her
mouth.*)

No cigarettes, please.

GOLDA: Look, without cigarettes I can't make it.

2ND: We may not make it with. Come.

(*He retires a few steps;* GOLDA *turns to us as sound
rises, the Arab chant of a muezzin; behind her,
actors move in silently with chairs, a rug, candles,
and create a room.*)

GOLDA: —ninety million Arabs around us, five times a
day on their faces praying to Allah for peace; and
the one I've been bundled into Transjordan to see,
in this schmotte, is—

ABDULLAH [ENTERS AT REAR]: Mrs. Myerson.

GOLDA [TURNS]: —King Abdullah.

ABDULLAH: You look charming, I am happy you crossed
safely. Please sit.

(*The Arabs disappear at* ABDULLAH's *gesture—he is
the* 1ST *Witness, a different role—and he sits;*
GOLDA *sits, and unveils her face.*)

GOLDA: I can't talk through a veil.

ABDULLAH [*smiles*]: It is why we like women to wear it, perhaps. We are not progressive; you Jews have been so innovative in Palestine, bringing the swamps and dunes to life; share your secrets with us.

GOLDA: It's one secret—

ABDULLAH: The easier.

GOLDA: —for two thousand years pray, Next year in Jerusalem.

ABDULLAH: Of course; only the spirit makes the world fruitful.

GOLDA: Work doesn't hurt.

ABDULLAH: You know my belief that Allah scattered the Jews throughout the West that they might bring its knowledge back to us?—since we are all the children of Shem—

GOLDA: Look, in five days it's war. And the children will murder each other.

(ABDULLAH *is silent.*)

You're breaking your promise to me?

ABDULLAH [*slowly*]: That promise I made in—

GOLDA: November.

ABDULLAH: Yes—

GOLDA: Before the UN vote to partition.

ABDULLAH: —and alone among my brothers of the Arab states I accepted the UN partition—

2ND: They're not your brothers, they're your enemies.

ABDULLAH: They are my brothers and my enemies. Their view is a different one; they see the Jews returning as Europeans, no longer Semites—

GOLDA: Their view we've heard—

ABDULLAH: —but invaders.

GOLDA: —from our brother, the head of the Arab League, "This will be a war of extermination—"

ABDULLAH: Yes.

GOLDA: "—and a momentous massacre, like the Mongol massacres."

ABDULLAH: Yes.

GOLDA: Are you joining them?—that's my question.

(ABDULLAH *is silent.*)

In the winter you sent me a message—

ABDULLAH: I remember it.

GOLDA: —you're a Bedouin and so a man of honor, and two, a King besides, and three, a promise to a woman you'd never break.

ABDULLAH: Such good reasons—

GOLDA: So many it worried us.

ABDULLAH: But then I was alone; now I am one of five nations. And no longer master of my own destiny.

GOLDA [PAUSE]: So the word I'll bring back is—

ABDULLAH: Mrs. Myerson, you can avert this massacre.

GOLDA: I would love to, how?

ABDULLAH: Do not proclaim your state.

GOLDA: No, no—

ABDULLAH: The Arab world cannot now accept a Jewish state in its midst, why are you in such a hurry?

GOLDA: Two thousand years I can't call a hurry.

ABDULLAH: Wait one more. I make you a new offer, now: I will annex Palestine, unpartitioned, and

merge it with Jordan; and after one year the Jews
will sit in my parliament.

GOLDA: As a minority.

ABDULLAH: Proportionally. I will treat you very well—
protect you—

GOLDA: Like the Germans?—fifty years you've seen us
here fighting the land—

ABDULLAH: I admire it.

GOLDA: —and Arab riots, fighting each other, fighting
the British army to smuggle in our survivors, there
isn't a Jew among us didn't give sweat or blood;
but to sit again in somebody else's parliament?—
that isn't what we dreamed.

ABDULLAH: It is a dream; I offer you a compromise that
is realizable.

GOLDA: Not ten Jews would stand for such a plan.

ABDULLAH [TURNS]: You are an Oriental Jew?

2ND: Yes.

ABDULLAH: Reason with her. Bring me an answer by
May 15th, to take to my Arab friends, and we can
live in peace.

2ND: You have no Arab friends, only us.

GOLDA: I can answer now. If it's war, we'll fight some
more—

ABDULLAH: It means the ruin of all you achieved in fifty
years—

GOLDA: —and we'll win.

(A *silence*.)

ABDULLAH: Is there anything more to be said?

(*He waits; then* GOLDA *stands.*)

GOLDA: Only shalom.

ABDULLAH [STANDS]: Salaam. There is so narrow a difference in how we say peace.

GOLDA: How many Jewish bodies will you bury in it?

(*She walks with the* 2ND *actor up left, where he helps her unrobe;* ABDULLAH *remains. Sound resumes, the muezzin's call to prayer.* ABDULLAH *goes to his palms and face, praying; actors remove the room things, and one—the* MOTHER, *but a different role—lingers on the platform up right as the* 3RD *Witness.*)

3RD WITNESS: Golda, companion of kings, well, she was Goldie Mabovitch when I went to school with her in Milwaukee, and she wanted to be a teacher. She had a very bossy mother said no, no high school, she could just keep working in the store with her; so she packed up her things, lowered them out the window one night to me, and next morning got on the train to Denver. Went to high school, lived with her sister, and in her kitchen met that whole crowd of Zionists, socialists, anarchists—and of course Morris. Long dead now. But then it turned out the sister was just as bossy as the mother, so Goldie moved out on her too; found a job doing skirt-linings, and was on her own, at sixteen. I mean, if there was ever one word for Goldie it has to be independent.

(Two actors in Arab headgear enter behind ABDUL-
LAH *praying.)*

So when a couple of years after her meeting with
King Abdullah she heard the news—

*(*ABDULLAH *rises, the two Arabs fire; he reels between them to escape, they follow shooting, and
he falls in the dark upstage; they run off.)*

—that he was assassinated, Goldie said, "And if
I'd said yes to his offer?"

(Lights out on her, and up on GOLDA's *office—the
1st actor in windbreaker and eyepatch facing her
across a desk map, the 4th in khaki listening.)*

1st: The Syrians are at Nafekh now.
GOLDA: What?
1st: Headquarters pulled out at 1:15, we're throwing in
     reserves piecemeal. Golda, I've never felt so anx-
     ious, if we don't understand the situation fast—

(He twists the map for her.)

Here, the Suez—the Egyptians have two thousand
tanks, we're holding the Canal with 280, we're
throwing in reserves piecemeal! Forget the Bar-Lev
line—it's gone—
GOLDA: You're telling me what, the whole front is col-
     lapsing?
1st: It may be, will be if we don't shorten the line—

4TH: Pull back?

1ST: We can't save the Bar-Lev forts—

GOLDA: Pull back to where?

1ST: First, evacuate all the Bar-Lev strongholds to-night—

4TH: Abandon the Canal?

1ST: —and withdraw to a new line a dozen kilometers back—

4TH: I mean to cross it.

1ST: Golda, ask Bar-Lev himself—

4TH: I have a counterattack shaping up.

1ST: —we can't push the Egyptians back now—

4TH: Of course we can. You've lost your confidence, Moshe.

1ST [SHAKEN]: If we try it and fail, the fate of Israel will be at stake.

(A *silence.* GOLDA *lights a cigarette.*)

GOLDA [STOLID]: Excuse me—

(*She leaves them in dimming light over the desk map, comes down from her office, and stands trembling with palms over her eyes;* LOU *comes in with a trayful, stops.*)

LOU: You're gray.

GOLDA: I think I'm going out of my senses. Moshe says it's a catastrophe, retreat—

LOU: No—

GOLDA [TO HERSELF]: The work of a lifetime? I'll kill myself first—

LOU: What?

GOLDA: If we lose this war, I'll kill myself, yes—

LOU [STARES]: You're serious.

GOLDA: —what they do to each other we know, think what they'll do to our Jews—

LOU: First, I have here only soup, not poisonous enough, and second, you cannot kill yourself before the election.

GOLDA [GRIM PAUSE]: Lose the election too I'll kill myself first and second. Ask Lior to find Bar-Lev.

(LOU *takes the tray up to the office, and sound comes in, shells exploding, half-intelligible voices on radio crackling*—)

—*Low on ammunition, sir, can I withdraw to reload?*

—*No. Use small arms.*

—*Tiger here, they're coming from the south, two thousand yards, about 40 of them.*

—*Hold fire till eight hundred.*

—*Only one shell per tank, sir.*

—*Give me another half hour, you'll be getting reinforcements, please hold on!*

—*Sir, I can't hold on.*

—*For God's sake, hold on for ten minutes, help's on the way*—

(—*until* GOLDA *half covers her ears and turns, going deep into herself; sound dies*—)

Didn't I know what an old invalid was good for?—

(—*into a solo cello playing Bach, the 5th Suite saraband; light changes into a green dapple of leaf-light—*)

—retired, five years ago in the garden—

(—*and a woman brings a chair down right;* GOLDA *sits, takes her hand—*)

—with my children, Sarile—

(—*and a boy and girl run in, to pose around* GOLDA's *feet for a smiling photo.*)

—and grandchildren. Menachem! we're ready—

(*Sound stops; a man comes to take his place, cello-bow in hand.*)

I made one mistake in my life—
MAN: Yes, mother.
GOLDA: —I should never have left the kibbutz. But now I have my own—
WOMAN: Hold still, momma.
BOY: Grandma, why are your legs different?
GOLDA: Who says they're different?
BOY: My eyes say, one is fatter—
GOLDA: Maybe one of your eyes is fatter.
BOY: Oh?—that's what philosophers call the subject-object relationship—
GOLDA: Three times a day I get an inferiority complex from him. Look, first I broke it, then it got phle-

bitis, then a lunatic threw a grenade into the old
Knesset and—

WOMAN: Hold still, momma.

BOY [SCRAMBLES UP]: The dog, get the dog—

GOLDA: About that dog I'm not as enthused as the dog
is about me—

(*But the group is slipping away as she glances,
disappearing in shadows—the woman last, letting
go of* GOLDA's *hand—*)

WOMAN: Momma—momma—

(*—until* GOLDA *sits alone, listening to a child's voice
call like an echo.*)

SMALL GIRL [OFF]: Momma—momma—

(*She turns in with a doll—dreamlike, clothes* 1930's
—not seeing GOLDA, *but spying a younger boy
opposite, who throws a strapful of schoolbooks on
the floor.*)

Menachem—

YOUNGER BOY: She's not here, stupid, so shut up.

SMALL GIRL: My dolly's sick, I want momma—

YOUNGER BOY: Let's call her. Mother!

SMALL GIRL, YOUNGER BOY [TOGETHER]: Momma!
Mother! Momma!

YOUNGER BOY [TAUNTING]: Ha ha, she's in Haifa at a
meeting.

SMALL GIRL [TEARFUL]: Momma—

(*She turns out;* morris *turns in, with a book.*)

morris: What's the difficulty here?

younger boy: There's nobody to carry my cello, where's
    mother?

morris: Ah, now cello lessons I approve, I'll help carry—

younger boy: I want *her*, here.

morris: Here I'm afraid she isn't.

younger boy: Where is she?

morris: In Geneva, at a meeting. Come, I'll—

younger boy: I want *her*, I want *her*—

morris: Menachem, dear—

(*The boy wheels away, the small girl turns in
opposite.*)

Sarile?

small girl: I didn't know you're visiting, poppa.

morris: Just—waiting to see your momma—

small girl: She's away.

morris: Oh. Where?

small girl: She's in New York at a meeting.

morris [depressed]: So. So.

golda [eyes closed]: Forgive me—forgive me—

morris: Well, should I read some more to you?—see,
    I brought for entertainment a masterpiece I think
    you'll both like—

younger boy: What's it about?

morris: Ideals. Listen, he tells right away.

(morris *settles cross-legged, with the book; the
children come to lie on their bellies.*)

"At a certain village in La Mancha, there lived not long ago one of those old-fashioned gentlemen who are never without a lance on a rack, an old target, and a skinny horse."

GOLDA [NOT TURNING]: What's wrong with ideals?

MORRIS [MILDLY]: What's wrong with the real world?

GOLDA: Everything; ideals are how we change it.

MORRIS: Children, here and now, that's an ideal too—

GOLDA: Morris, I want them to grow up in a world that's safe.

MORRIS: I want them to grow up with a mother, Goldie. How do you feel when they're sick and need you?

GOLDA [PAUSE]: Guilty. Whatever I do. To them, to the cause—

(*The* 2ND *actor enters down left;* LOU *is in the office.*)

2ND [THE DRAWLER]: I'm told the Lady sent for me—

LOU: She's down the hall.

(GOLDA *rises heavily.*)

MORRIS: Such a stateswoman—

GOLDA: Bar-Lev, I need eyes!

MORRIS: —your hands full of everything except them—

GOLDA: Could you do me a big favor?—

(*The lights lose* MORRIS *and the children.*)

2ND: I'll try.

GOLDA: —leave your own department?

2ND: The supermarkets are mobbed, Golda, I'm—calming the panic.

GOLDA: Calm mine.

(The 4TH actor comes in, with memos.)

4TH: Golda—

2ND [APPRAISES HER]: You're a rock.

4TH: —I must hold onto the Canal, our defense is counterattack.

GOLDA [TO 2ND]: I don't like what I hear.

4TH: Fall back to a new line and—

GOLDA: —you can't counterattack.

4TH: Not and cross the Canal.

2ND: Tell me what I can do.

GOLDA: Fly up to the Golan tonight, talk with the commanders there. Look, how soon would you counterattack on the Suez?

4TH [GIVES HER THE MEMOS]: How soon will you get me the replacements I lose?

GOLDA: The minute Dinitz gets to Washington.

4TH: It depends, I have to see if Bren's division—

GOLDA: So go down and see! Chaim, fly up now and tell me what *you* think.

(She walks him left.)

Also why an army retires its best generals to the supermarkets—

2ND: Let's turn back the Arabs first.

GOLDA: Yes, after we win.

(*The* 2ND *leaves, left; the* 4TH *lingers, right.*)

4TH: Golda.
GOLDA: You're still here?
4TH: I salute you.

(*He goes out;* LOU *remains.*)

LOU: And how much poison am I to order, my dear
    lady?
GOLDA: Enough for both of us.
LOU: Oh?
GOLDA: But we'll wait till tomorrow.

(*She trudges up to her office, to read the memos;
the lighting explodes, in a flood of orange fire-
glare; then slowly fades—*)

LOU: Soviet missiles.

(*—and* LOU *turns down left, another Witness.*)

I went to Moscow with Golda in '48, when she was
our first Ambassador. But how to meet the Jews
of Russia after thirty years we didn't see; even
relatives we were afraid to contact, for their sake,
Zionism was a crime—

(GOLDA *picks up her phone—*)

GOLDA: Get me Dinitz.

(—*and replaces it.*)

LOU: —and in the Moscow synagogue only a handful of
    shabby old Jews would still come. So Golda said on
    Rosh Hashanah the entire legation would go, and
    we notified the Rabbi, and that day in the street of
    the synagogue we were mobbed by fifty thousand
    Jews, old men and women, teenagers, Red Army
    soldiers, mothers with babies, stretching out hands
    and calling in Yiddish, Goldele, Goldele, leben
    zolst du, Goldele, and when the cantor saw the
    Star of David on our military attaché's hat he
    shrieked!—the colonel's son ran away with the hat
    under his coat to save it, and to those thousands
    and thousands of Jews blowing her kisses, crying,
    kissing her dress, Golda said one sentence, A dank
    eich vos ihr seit geblieben Yidden, Thank you for
    remaining Jews.

(*Down right the* 5TH *actor in a topcoat sits with
a phone in the chair;* GOLDA's *phone rings.*)

A photograph of the crowd was taken by a twelve-
year-old boy with a birthday camera—

GOLDA: Yes?

5TH: Mrs. Meir—Hello, hello—Operator—

LOU: —and for weeks people on the street would whisper
    to us, I have the picture, I have the picture—

GOLDA [TESTY]: No, I'll hold.

LOU: —and copies travelled everywhere. In Siberia a
    girl from Vilna, sentenced to work in the lumber

woods, was at the fire warming her chunk of frozen bread when she saw a man spying on her among the trees; he said, Are you Jewish? and she said yes, and out of his rags he took the torn picture and whispered, There is a Jewish state—

5TH: Mrs. Meir?

GOLDA: Simcha.

5TH: I'm here. Finally, what a trip—

LOU [OVER]: And after thirty years the Soviets knew they still had a Jewish problem.

GOLDA: You saw Kissinger?

(LOU *leaves; lights up on* GOLDA *and the* 5TH.)

5TH: At six o'clock. I just left him—

GOLDA: And the Phantoms?

5TH: He knows we didn't preempt and approves, he says it was the right decision—

GOLDA: A medal I don't need. Phantoms are enough.

5TH: I said yes but it laid a heavy responsibility on his government—

GOLDA: So when do we get them?

5TH: He has to check it out with the Pentagon. I'm to—

GOLDA: Check what, Nixon himself promised me.

5TH: It's a mess here, the police are on Agnew's doorstep, Nixon is locked up with his tapes, nobody—

GOLDA [FLAT]: Simcha.

5TH: Yes.

GOLDA: Get the Phantoms.

5TH: Of course, of course. I'm to call him—

GOLDA: Tell him we lost planes today like flies. Dado gives me here a new list, tanks also, spare parts,

electronic things, you'll have it in the morning.

5TH: I'll do everything I—

GOLDA: Simcha, half of this war is being fought by you. Such a thought frightens you?

5TH: Yes.

GOLDA: Good.

(*She hangs up; lights out on the* 5TH *actor, who moves the chair up right as he leaves; down left a bodyguard—the* 4TH *actor, a different role—brings in a chair and sits,* GOLDA *scowling at the memos.*)

And in my old age I'm in the munitions business?

(*She flings them down on the desk, pauses in a reach for cigarettes, heavily.*)

The Jewish homeland must be a model for the redemption of the human race, who said it?— Ben-Gurion, Milwaukee, 1916. I heard him, did any of us dream of this killing?

(*Her pack is empty, she slaps it on the desk, and marches to the office edge, lighter in hand.*)

Is anybody down there?

BODYGUARD: Just me, Golda.

GOLDA [TRUDGES DOWN]: Hymie, I'm all out again.

BODYGUARD [RISES]: Sure, here.

(GOLDA *takes a cigarette from his pack; lights down on the office.*)

Why don't you let me drive you home and get a
night's sleep?

GOLDA: Who will answer the phone—

BODYGUARD: Keep them, I got more in the car.

(*She lights it.*)

First time I drove you, remember?—

GOLDA: No.

BODYGUARD: —to be sworn in? you sat in the front seat,
I said, Mrs. Meir, please sit in the back seat, you're
the Prime Minister now, you said, I didn't do anything yet.—Things have changed.

GOLDA: Yes.

BODYGUARD: I'll check outside.

GOLDA: Yes—

(*He goes out;* GOLDA *sits heavily in the chair, eyes
closed, going into herself; the lights change to
memory.*)

—things have changed. 1917, 18—rid of the Kaiser
and Czar, no more tyrants, peace and socialism—
Oh, like a young girl this century was, such a
beauty—

(MORRIS *in 1915 garb stands in the shadows behind
the chair up right.*)

—and so much evil in her, Stalin, the depression,
Hitler, World War II, the Holocaust, the atom
bomb—

MORRIS: Where did it come from—

GOLDA: It looked so easy, sweep out the leftovers—

MORRIS: —the evil?

GOLDA: —build a new land with young people, hard workers, happy—

MORRIS: You did think be happy once. 1915—

GOLDA [NOT TURNING]: For everybody, yes.

MORRIS: —in Milwaukee again, you wrote a postcard to—

GOLDA: No.

MORRIS: —yes, I remember on the back—

GOLDA: No.

MORRIS: "You'll never guess who arrived last night— Morris—"

GOLDA: No.

MORRIS: "— I'm the happiest person alive."

GOLDA [EYES CLOSED]: Yes.

MORRIS: And I said, Goldie—

(*He comes around the chair up right to sit shyly,* GOLDA *in the chair down left not turning, each in a separate pool of light; they talk looking straight ahead, dreamlike.*)

—by letter is no way, Goldie, I'm tired of living with you in a mailbox.

GOLDA: Oh, Morris, I've told you I love you—

MORRIS: I want us to be married now.

GOLDA: —but there's something else now.

MORRIS: Who?

(*The* MOTHER *and a teen-age* CLARA—*the sister—
come down right, bearing platters and chairs to set
the platform as a table; lights on it.*)

MOTHER [SHOUTS]: Supper, Moishe! Clara, get your
poppa.

CLARA [SHOUTS]: Poppa! Supper!

GOLDA [REMAINS LEFT]: Momma, this is Morris Myerson, from Denver. I invited him.

MORRIS: I'm very pleased to meet—

MOTHER: And what does he do for a living?

MORRIS: I'm a sign-painter, I—

MOTHER: Mr. Goodstein owns a real-estate office—

MORRIS: —paint signs—

MOTHER: —but take a bite with us, Meyer.

GOLDA: Mr. Goodstein is an old man.

MOTHER [INDIGNANT]: Old!

GOLDA: In his *thirties*, momma.

(*The* FATHER—*the* 3RD *actor—comes in shaking
leaflets;* MORRIS *brings his chair; all sit, and will
address an empty place as* GOLDA.)

MOTHER: Moishe, this is Meyer Morrison, from Denver.

MORRIS: Myerson.

MOTHER: He wrote the letters.

MORRIS: Schubert when he died left eleven dollars.

FATHER: What?

MORRIS [GENTLY]: He owned a music office—in his
head—

GOLDA: Morris dear, money isn't the thing.

FATHER [THE LEAFLETS]: Look, Blume, all over the street
   by the synagogue—

MOTHER: Eat, everybody—

MOTHER, CLARA [TOGETHER]: —it shouldn't get cold.

MORRIS: Goldie, let me not to the marriage of true
   minds admit impediment.

FATHER: What?

MORRIS: Love is not love which alters when it alteration
   finds—

GOLDA: What, Morris?

FATHER [BAFFLED]: Not a word he says!

MORRIS: The sonnets?—they're very high on the list
   I sent.

GOLDA: Morris, the list was so long—

FATHER [THE LEAFLETS]: See, a spectacle she's making
   of me!

MOTHER: Eat, eat—

MOTHER, CLARA [TOGETHER]: —we'll fight later.

FATHER: No daughter of Moishe Mabovith on a soap-
   box outside the synagogue is making speeches!

GOLDA: Look, *in* the synagogue they don't let me talk—

FATHER: When you're a man you'll talk *in* the synagogue!—so wait. You hear?

GOLDA: Deaf I'm not, poppa, just female.

FATHER: Good. It's not a nice thing, Goldie, a girl on a
   box—

GOLDA: I'm talking tonight. On a streetcorner.

FATHER: On a box?

GOLDA: All the comrades are meeting me there.

FATHER: *I'll* meet you!—and drag you home in the
   street—

GOLDA: Poppa, I promised!

FATHER: —by the braid! You heard it?—tonight you stay
home or by the braid!

(*He contemplates* MORRIS.)

Denver.

MORRIS: Yes.

FATHER: So what are you doing in Milwaukee?

MORRIS: Marrying Goldie.

(*The parents stiffen; a silence.*)

GOLDA: The thing is, I don't want to be "Morris's
wife"—

MOTHER [RELIEVED]: Ah—

GOLDA: —and don't want not to be Morris's wife.

FATHER [NOT RELIEVED]: Oh?

MORRIS: It's a bissel not clear.

GOLDA: I mean women live so *small*, stuck in the
kitchen, and outside the whole world is calling us
to come change it—

MORRIS: Goldie child, for thousands of years men have
been changing the world, always for the worse.

GOLDA: —how can I just make motza-balls?—in Pinsk
this year by the old church Petlura stood the Jews
up and shot them—families we knew—

MORRIS: It's very different here.

GOLDA: Here?—we'll disappear.

MORRIS: So perhaps we should, it's nature's way with
the superfluous.

GOLDA: And marry you here *I'll* disappear.

(*A silence; the parents relax.*)

FATHER: Good. Meyer—

MORRIS: Morris.

FATHER: —the letters we read—

GOLDA: What?

MOTHER: Moishe!

FATHER: —not exactly read—

GOLDA: What letters?

MOTHER: Everybody knows in English I can't read—

GOLDA: What letters?

CLARA [JUMPS UP]: The letters Morris wrote you—
Goldie, I swear I didn't want to—

MORRIS: You read *our* letters?

FATHER: Just yours.

MOTHER: —not read even, Clara told them to me in
Yiddish—

CLARA: She made me, Goldie—

MOTHER: What's happening to my daughter I have to
know!

CLARA: —but I left out the best parts—

FATHER: The point is—

GOLDA [COLDLY]: Clara, it's not what socialists do.

CLARA: Oh, I hate everybody—

(*She runs out in tears; the* MOTHER *rises to go
after her.*)

MOTHER: Fight, fight—we'll eat later—

FATHER: The point is, we know you from the letters,
Meyer, and the answer is no.

GOLDA: The answer is yes!—I'll give the answer—

GOLDA

MOTHER [OFF]: Moishe, come out here this minute, you
—you—

FATHER: Excuse me.

MOTHER: —naarische kopf!

(*The* FATHER *hurries out;* MORRIS *stands behind*
GOLDA.)

MORRIS: So it's yes.

GOLDA: No, it's maybe. Morris, you're a wonderful
person, and know everything I don't, but a life
so squeezed in?—oh, someday there'll be a world
where poor Jews open up like flowers, no meanness,
no war, no disease or capitalist inequality—

MORRIS [DRY]: Someday. Meanwhile?

GOLDA: I want a part in building it. The women there
are ploughing the land, sharing with the men the
dangers and hard work—

(*The* MOTHER *and* CLARA *return, to clear off, but
leaving the chairs.*)

MORRIS: Women where?

GOLDA: —Rachel Bluwstein, Rachel Yanait—

MORRIS: Who?

GOLDA: —in Palestine, pioneers. New women, wives and
mothers they are also—

MORRIS: Palestine.

GOLDA: —but not just.

MORRIS: You want to go to Palestine—

GOLDA: A parlor Zionist I don't—

MORRIS: —not marry me?

GOLDA: I want to marry you *and* go to Palestine.

MORRIS: Goldie, I like the city, concerts, libraries, I
     don't like rocks and Arabs. Here I can find work,
     a little flat—and a quiet wedding, a judge, no
     chuppah, not religious, just—

MOTHER [TURNS]: No chuppah!

MORRIS: Mrs. Mabovitch, you see we're—

MOTHER: I'll kill myself, no chuppah—

GOLDA: Momma.

MOTHER: —in a dogcatcher's office you'll get married?—

MORRIS: —very enlightened socialists, but—

MOTHER: —the Rebbeh will spit me in the face—

MORRIS: —if a chuppah is so important—

MOTHER: I'll leave the city!

GOLDA: Momma, there maybe won't be a wedding!

MOTHER [WILDLY]: Why are you doing this to me?

(*She marches out,* CLARA *following;* MORRIS *is alone
with* GOLDA.)

MORRIS: Goldie, dear revolutionary, if your poppa won't
     allow you out to the streetcorner?—Palestine isn't
     so near—

GOLDA: I'm going tonight to the streetcorner.

MORRIS: At seventeen, don't—make up your mind—

GOLDA: And to Palestine whenever.

(MORRIS *stands, unhappy.*)

MORRIS: Goldie child, I don't want to plough the land.
     The spirit I—envy, but human beings suffer, if they
     suffer in Jerusalem instead of Pinsk is that better?

(*A pause.*)

I'm—not the happiest person alive—

(*He turns out, the lights dimming on him; sound rises—one air-raid siren wailing—and lights up on* GOLDA's *lamp-lit office and the* 2ND *actor in army windbreaker; she trudges up.*)

2ND [DRAWING]: It's not hopeless, Golda. You want the details?

GOLDA: Of course.

2ND: We held on by our eyelids today—

(*He marks the desk-map.*)

—they took Nafekh, we took it back; they got as far as Snobar here—

GOLDA: Ach.

2ND: —five minutes from the Jordan. Now, can we knock them off balance?—the reserves are up, Musa's 14th on the El Al road, Laner with four brigades here at Yehudia and Aleika. If we counterattack—in a pincers, so—

GOLDA: When?

2ND: In the morning. It's dangerous, a one-to-three ratio we accept, we're fighting one-to-five; we need Dado's consent—

GOLDA: Dado called an hour ago.

2ND: Oh?

GOLDA: He's counterattacking on the Suez.

2ND: When?

GOLDA: In the morning. We're fighting on three fronts—

2ND: Three?

GOLDA: Egypt, Syria, and time. Eban expects at the UN
a Soviet move for a cease-fire, to freeze the lines.

2ND: So they start nearer, next time?

GOLDA: I said no. Chaim, will you come back to the
army, take a command again?

2ND: If it's a real command.

GOLDA: Dado will consent. Do you pray?

2ND: Do you?

GOLDA: I'll try anything.

(*She gathers up folders from the desk—*)

Nu, Goldele, so clever—

(*—and puts out the lamp; they begin to descend.*)

My mother Blume would prove God exists—

2ND: How?

GOLDA: —why else does it rain?—so from a schoolbook
I explained meteorology; she said, Nu, Goldele, if
you're so clever you make it rain.

2ND: Rain won't help.

GOLDA: What will?

2ND: Killing them.

GOLDA [LONG PAUSE]: In heaven I'll—maybe—forgive
them for killing our boys; one thing I'll never
forgive—

2ND: What?

GOLDA: —making us kill theirs.

(*She dumps the folders on the chair, moves it up center as lights die, and sits; the* 2ND *actor leaves, and up right the* 3RD *brings another chair down center, places it reversed, and comes down front as the* 4TH *Witness, a different role.*)

4TH WITNESS: Golda?—Rachel weeping for her children, and if you're in her way get off the earth. I sat on a UJA committee with her in New York, debating all day do we add an extra twenty-five million or fifty to the drive, earmarked for Israel, what's realistic?—we voted twenty-five, secret ballot, by one vote. Done with?—no. Golda said, I want to know how everybody voted. So man by man she went around the table, how did you vote? how did you vote? and a sweetheart I'll call Harvey, who's devoted his life to Israel, was the one she picked; she slid him a note. He read it, and went white. Golda walked out. I ran after to stop her at the elevator, she broke away, said, No, no, it's your fault, you're no good, and rode down. I went back, and the note was shaking in Harvey's hands, it said, Your vote is a vote for the Arabs.

(*In the dark behind him the other actors—the* 4TH *in army khaki—come in separately with folders to move the supper chairs.*)

He's been carrying that note in his wallet for years, waiting for her to take it back.

(*He turns to join the others; sound explodes—*

a huge cacophony of war, all-out—while the five
actors seat themselves downstage from GOLDA *as*
around a circular table in cabinet meeting.)

(*Lights up, sound dies, the talk becoming audible*
—the 5TH *actor, in a different role.*)

5TH [WITH A FOLDER]: —and figure the cost at ten billion
pounds. So, first a compulsory war loan of one
billion. On income, a sliding tax, from 7 per cent
up to 12—you have the figures—interest at 3 per
cent, refunded in fifteen years. Second, a voluntary
war loan of another billion, the response is already
tremendous. And third, abroad. I leave this week
for fund-raising, Europe and the States.

(*He closes the folder;* GOLDA *looks around*).

GOLDA: Anybody?—So, the front lines. Moshe?
1ST: The chief of staff—

(*The* 4TH *actor rises sombrely, stands a map on*
the reversed chair, and talks from it.)

4TH: First priority, the Golan news is better. Very
heavy fighting, but from Juhader we're closing this
pincers; if we can clean out the Hushniyah pocket
tomorrow we'll push them back to the UN line,
but it's no rout. Yesterday on the Suez—
1ST: Everything went wrong.
4TH: —we ran into a stone wall. Worse, orders got con-

fused, the attack developed not down their north
flank—

5TH: Orders got confused?

4TH: War gets confused, yes—

2ND: What happened?

4TH: We went straight into the teeth of the bridgehead
—antitank missiles, thousands of infantry, Katyusha
rockets, artillery—an inferno. We sent tanks in
like cavalry without air support—we couldn't get
through the missiles—and they took heavy losses.
And we lost a number of positions here in the
Hamutal area. It was a very bad day, we can't
afford another one like it.

(*A silence.*)

GOLDA [LOW]: You have casualty figures?

4TH: Not yet. High, high.

GOLDA [PAUSE]: You plan what?

4TH: Hold, and let them have losses attacking us. On
the positive side, here we found the boundary
between their Second and Third armies, and it's
soft. That's all.

(*He sits; the* 1ST *rises.*)

1ST: Two points. First, the Suez command is fighting
among itself—

GOLDA: What?

4TH: Gonen's asked me to relieve Sharon.

GOLDA: No. Sharon?—

4TH: A sonofabitch to get on with, but—

GOLDA: —what a fighter—

1ST: We need a new commander down there—

4TH: Agreed.

1ST: —and our choice is Bar-Lev. Second, the war itself. Materiel is being squandered on counterattacks, and no help from the Americans to make up our losses—

GOLDA: Some items in the pipeline we'll get, Dinitz says Kissinger is sympathetic, but—

1ST: Then what's the delay?

GOLDA: Kissinger has other interests besides us. What's he thinking? —detente, don't offend Brezhnev, oil, Faisal is talking embargo, Watergate, the White House is already shaky, Vietnam, another one they can't have—

1ST: Some units are fighting with their last shells.

GOLDA: —so I have to see a way.

1ST: In three days we've lost 10 per cent of the air force, how many hundreds of tanks?—we can't throw them back now. We *can* retreat to new lines they can't cross.

(*He waits.*)

Yes or no?

4TH: That's what you'll say on TV tonight?

1ST: It's the truth.

GOLDA: You're on TV tonight?

1ST: Yes.

(A *silence;* GOLDA *rises heavily.*)

GOLDA: Sunday is Ben-Gurion's birthday, we'll send him
    a greeting?
3RD: I'll draft it—

   (*The meeting breaks up, some leaving with chairs,
   some standing in gloomy conversation; the* 1ST
   catches GOLDA *downstage.*)

1ST: Golda, I'd like an answer.
GOLDA: Do me a favor.
1ST: Of course.
GOLDA: Don't go on TV tonight.
1ST: Why?
GOLDA: You'll be terrible for morale.
1ST: The country has a right to the truth.
GOLDA: Stay home tonight or by the braids.
1ST: What?
GOLDA: Nothing, an old head's full of things, I'll send
    Yariv instead.
1ST: Is that your answer?

   (GOLDA *stands with eyes closed; light fades on the
   others, as they leave, and changes to memory—*)

GOLDA [SLOWLY]: Stones—
1ST [RECEDING]: What?
GOLDA [INTO HERSELF]: —in 1948 our answer was
    stones—

   (*—while backlighting silhouettes on the platform
   up right a man on a chair, the* 1ST *Witness as* BEN-
   GURION, *half averted.*)

BEN-GURION: Is Kaplan right?—he's just back.

GOLDA [NOT TURNING]: What does he say?

BEN-GURION: Not more than six million from American Jews, don't count on it.

GOLDA: Why?

BEN-GURION: They're sick of us. Goldie, I wake up in a sweat, what's going to happen to us?—the British leave, the Arabs will attack, we have nothing.

GOLDA: The Haganah is nothing?

BEN-GURION: Do you know what the Haganah has cached away?—

GOLDA: Not to the—

BEN-GURION: —ten thousand rifles, not two thousand Sten guns. Sixty mortars, they make a noise. Against five armies?—I don't sleep, what's going to happen to us?

(GOLDA *drops her folders on the bed-platform down right, picks up from it a handbag.*)

GOLDA [SLOWLY]: I haven't been there in ten years—

BEN-GURION [TO HIMSELF]: Tanks I can get in Czechoslovakia for ten million—ammunition another ten—

GOLDA: —but I speak a good American.

BEN-GURION: I must go, yes.

GOLDA: Where?

BEN-GURION: To the Jews of the States.

GOLDA: Leave here now? Look, what you can do here I can't; there—?

BEN-GURION: I must go myself.

GOLDA: B. G., it's out of the question.

BEN-GURION [SUDDENLY]: All right. Go today.

GOLDA: My coat's in Jerusalem—

BEN-GURION: Don't even go back to Jerusalem.

> (*The lights lose* BEN-GURION, *unmoving, and* GOLDA
> *comes center with her handbag to face us; a girl
> from left meets her with a cloth coat, drapes it
> over her shoulders.*)

GIRL: Welcome to America, Mrs. Myerson.

GOLDA: Thank you, Fanny, where's my sister?

> (CLARA—*middle-aged,* LOU *in a different role—
> hurries in from right.*)

CLARA: Goldie, Goldie!

GOLDA: Clara.

> (*They embrace.*)

Clara, I must talk with Henry Montor.

CLARA: He's in Chicago.

GOLDA: What's in Chicago?

CLARA: The Council of Jewish Federations, they're
meeting day after tomorrow—Goldie, you should
talk there!

GOLDA: Could I?

GIRL: It's not Zionist, Mrs. Myerson.

GOLDA: Call him. See.

GIRL: It's for the communities here, welfare, new hos-
pitals, temples—

GOLDA: It's *all* the Jews.

CLARA: Yes, pro, anti—

GOLDA: Call him.

(CLARA *and the girl leave;* GOLDA *remains facing us; a chairman steps in, right.*)

CHAIRMAN: Friends. We have with us today an unexpected visitor from Palestine, who has asked time for a few words. She is currently on the executive of the Jewish Agency there, Mrs. Goldie Myerson.

(*He leaves;* GOLDA *stands center with the handbag, in the coat. Lights fade to around* GOLDA.)

GOLDA: I have no speech. I'll tell you what's in my heart.

Fifty-four days ago the UN voted to partition Palestine—an Arab state, a Jewish state—thirty-three nations for, thirteen against. It wasn't the real vote. Six million corpses crying out in the graveyard of Europe cast the real vote.

That night I spoke from the balcony of my office in Jerusalem, to hundreds of Jews hugging, singing, dancing; I talked to the Arabs. "The plan is a compromise, not what you wanted, not what we wanted. But now let's live in friendship together." On another balcony an Arab lady said to a newspaperman from America, "Let them dance, they'll all soon be dead anyhow."

Next day seven Jews were killed in an Arab ambush on a bus. Two days later an Arab crowd set the

Jewish center of Jerusalem on fire. Not a week goes by without a horror.

I didn't come to the States only to save seven hundred thousand Jews after we've lost six million. But if the seven hundred thousand in Palestine can keep alive, then the Jewish people as such is alive. If they're killed off too, we're through with the dream of a Jewish people.

In May the British pull out, and five nations wait to massacre us. If we have arms to fight with, we'll fight with them. If not, we'll fight with stones.

The question is what can we get immediately— I don't mean two months from now, I don't mean next month. I mean now. I've come to tell you that within a very short period, a couple of weeks, we must have in cash twenty-five million dollars.

We've never told American Jews what to do. But you have two choices; we have only one.

You cannot decide whether we should fight or not. We will. That decision is taken. Nobody can change it. You can decide only one thing, whether we will live.

And I beg of you—don't be bitterly sorry three months from now for what you failed to do today.

(*Silence.* GOLDA *stands, while the girl comes to take the coat, leaves; lights silhouette* BEN-GURION *on his platform.*)

BEN-GURION [RISES]: Fifty million dollars—

GOLDA: For guns.

BEN-GURION: Goldie, when history is written, it will say
    there was a Jewish woman got the money that
    made the state possible.

GOLDA: For guns. Change the world—

(BEN-GURION *goes off.*)

—it changes you; something—wicked's in things;
that's the dybbuk.

(*She goes to the bed-platform, sits, picks up her
phone—*)

Dinitz. . . .

(*—and lights a cigarette. Up right the* 5TH *Witness
—the* 1ST *actor, a different role—comes to the chair
on the platform.*)

5TH WITNESS: Golda, of course, I sit across from her in
    the Knesset; she's a fossil. I'm not one of her
    admirers. I don't mean the hypocrisy—as Foreign
    Minister she broke men for sleeping around, if
    she slept with someone it was for the cause—but
    this war was predictable. Jews are standing with
    guns over an occupied people, why?—

GOLDA: . . . No, tell him call me as soon as he's back,
    I want to come see Nixon myself, incognito.

(*She hangs up.*)

5TH WITNESS: —because the Lady hasn't changed since
she was thirteen, it's them or us, the world is rotten
and hates Jews, she's so calcified there's a joke,
she won't take yes for an answer.

GOLDA [TO HERSELF]: Still for guns. Tell me—

(*She stubs out the cigarette, looks skyward—*)

—my friend, in the grain of this world you made,
so deep a twist of evil, in all of us. What for?

(*—waits—*)

Top secret.

(*—and lies down heavily with a blanket, in her
clothes; the dying lights focus on her. The* 5TH
Witness takes up the chair—)

5TH WITNESS: Doubts?—she sleeps like a rock.

(*—and goes off. The lights on* GOLDA *dreaming
linger, still linger; and then on the platform above
her they find the small girl again as before, sound
steals in around her—hoof-beats, rising into shouts,
windows smashing, a pogrom—and the girl stands
screaming; until the lights lose* GOLDA, *and the girl
too.*)

ACT II

GOLDA: Simcha—

5TH: —no, I've discussed it with him, and I think it's the last thing they want.

GOLDA: Why?

5TH: It embarrasses them; a visit by you in wartime—

(*Lights pick them out as they come downstage to take up their phones, the* 5TH *actor sitting to his down right,* GOLDA *at her desk with a cigarette.*)

—will identify them with us so openly it's a provocation—

GOLDA: Incognito, who'll know?

5TH: —to the Soviet Union. Kissinger says how can we keep you incognito?—

GOLDA [BITTERLY]: I'll wear my Arab outfit.

5TH: —and a visit's not necessary because the President already approves in principle all our requests.

GOLDA: What's that mean, in principle?

5TH: It means whenever the Pentagon can charter civilian planes to—

GOLDA: Ich ver meshugah duh, *where are the things?*

5TH: Golda, you have no idea the red tape I'm—

GOLDA: Boys are dying here! Call Kissinger back.

5TH: I can't call anybody now, it's three o'clock in the morning here.

GOLDA: Wake him up, does he know the Soviets are airlifting to Damascus?—

5TH: Yes.

GOLDA: —where are they chartering planes, Eskimos—

5TH: Golda, all I do is run between the White House and State Department and this Embassy, I'm sleeping here, I haven't been—

GOLDA [HARSH]: Everybody's sleeping there!

5TH: I can't call anybody till dawn.

GOLDA: All right. All right. Let's go back to '56—

5TH: '56.

GOLDA: —I was four months at the UN fighting off Eisenhower and Dulles, we went to a senator named Lyndon Johnson—

5TH: He's dead.

GOLDA: —who wrote a letter in the *New York Times*.

5TH: [PAUSE]: Ah.

GOLDA: The White House is walking five tightropes, a big tsimmis it can't have—

5TH: You want me to go public?—in the press?

GOLDA: I want you to say we'll go public.

5TH: There's a difference between saying and—

GOLDA: Of course, of course, we'll save the difference, what time is it?

5TH: Three o'clock.

GOLDA: Sleep till seven.

(She hangs up, busies herself over papers; the 5TH actor leaves as the 3RD in khaki comes in to GOLDA's office with letters.)

3RD: This I think you should see.

GOLDA [NOT LOOKING UP]: They're waiting downstairs.

3RD: From a mother in a kibbutz—

GOLDA: I can't now.

3RD: —with two sons, both killed Saturday.

(GOLDA raises her head; the 3RD proffers the letter.)

In the Golan.

GOLDA: Read it.

3RD: Just the end. ". . . happy boys and wanted very much to live and didn't hear what their general said yesterday, You have saved the people of Israel. Mommele Golda, don't cry for us. Be brave."

GOLDA [PAUSE]: Leave it.

3RD: You want me to answer?

GOLDA: I'll answer it.

(The 3RD goes out; GOLDA puts on glasses, reads, while from up right a woman comes to place a chair at center—another Witness, SARILE from the garden scene.)

SARILE: '56. That October my mother—Golda Meir now, Ben-Gurion had just made her Hebrew— spent a weekend I won't forget in Revivim. It's the kibbutz my husband and I helped start in the

Negev in the early '40's, nothing then, not a tree,
not a bird, for a year we lived in a cave, and the
water we drilled for was salty, we drank it for *ten*
years—people say so offhand we made the desert
bloom—but in '56 the trees were young; that weekend my mother played with her grandchildren
under them. She was Foreign Minister then, with
a secret to keep. On Monday war would break
out, and the Egyptian Army *could* strike back
through our kibbutz; her grandchildren were in its
path. She went back to Jerusalem without a word.
The war began the next day, and was over in a
week; and after when I said, But momma, why
didn't you warn me? she said, I couldn't tell everybody, how could I tell one?

(*She leaves;* LOU *enters below left to meet a two-
man TV team—the* 1ST *Witness and* 2ND *actor,
different roles—coming in from right with an ash-
tray-stand for the chair.*)

LOU: No ashtray.

TV INTERVIEWER: You're joking.

LOU: She doesn't smoke on television.

TV INTERVIEWER: Must be the one place, kill it. You
    heard the latest?

LOU [COOL]: I think so.

TV INTERVIEWER: No, Golda and Nixon are compliment-
    ing each other's foreign ministers, Golda says but
    Kissinger is so smart, Nixon says but Eban is so
    cultured, Golda says but of course we both have
    Jews, Nixon says but yours speaks better English—

(GOLDA *by now has come down, letter in hand.*)

Right here, Mrs. Meir. Five minutes?

(GOLDA *nods, sits; the light floods her.*)

I'll stay off-camera, a few questions—
GOLDA: The lights are too hot.
TV INTERVIEWER: I'm sorry, we have to see you, I
   promise it's not—
GOLDA: People shouldn't see me sweating, it'll worry
   them. Turn them down.
TV INTERVIEWER: You won't sweat; if they can't see
   you, sharp and clear—
GOLDA: What's more important?
TV INTERVIEWER: Mrs. Meir, trust me. Ready? We'll—

(GOLDA *gets up, walks away left.*)

Cut them in half!

(*The light is cut;* GOLDA *comes back, sits.*)

Better?

(GOLDA *nods.*)

You have a statement?
GOLDA: I'll make one.
TV INTERVIEWER: Ready?—Go.
GOLDA [TO THE CAMERA]: I'm able to tell you today the
   Golan Heights are back in our hands.

I want to stress not who but what we're fighting against. Thirty years the British army tried to hold down two thousand years of Jewish hopes; they couldn't. Nobody will. It's a promise, written in the Torah—and in the stars—to homeless people, you'll find your way home again. I mean all people, including our neighbors, there's no question that can't be settled if they grant us one right. To exist here.

For six years one of the two strongest nations in the world has been supplying them with arms— rockets, tanks, planes—the most sophisticated weapons to kill with, and this all in the name of socialist ideals. But if human life doesn't matter, what do you have ideals for?

The war isn't over. When it does end, it will end in victory.

TV INTERVIEWER: Madam Prime Minister, in a Jordanian communique today there was word of mobilization there. Will Jordan enter the war?

GOLDA: I don't know. I can say only this, an intelligent leader—once before he was asked not to enter a war—should have a good memory.

TV INTERVIEWER: You didn't mention the Egyptian front.

GOLDA: There we are holding, close to the Canal.

TV INTERVIEWER: Will we cross it?

GOLDA [DRY]: We haven't been invited.

TV INTERVIEWER: Can you say at this stage what our objectives are in this war?

GOLDA: Peace.

TV INTERVIEWER: The Soviet Union is calling for a cease-fire in place—

GOLDA: But on lines that don't mean they can regroup for a new attack.

TV INTERVIEWER: It's rumored the United States also favors—

GOLDA: I can't talk for any other government; we won't accept a cease-fire in place. If we had word they were ready to go back to the October 5th lines, we wouldn't lose many minutes in letting them.

TV INTERVIEWER: A question in the public mind, what is the price of this war?

GOLDA: Price?—every son who falls. That's a terrible price.

TV INTERVIEWER: Thank you, Mrs.—

GOLDA: I want to say a word to the mothers.

We're a small country, and one death a whole kibbutz weeps for; if five boys from Jerusalem die, there's not a family in the city doesn't know one of them.

Jews have always lived close to death, and love life the more; even in our religion there's not a law that can't be broken to save one life.

The chosen people never meant to me God chose us, it meant we chose him. It put us at the danger-point of everything human. Who knows more about suffering and love and exile and trying— we didn't always succeed—to live by the word we gave the world?

Israel was never just a country, it's a—human frontier, and that's what we've given our lives to.

And sometimes for.

TV INTERVIEWER [WAITS]: Thank you—

(*The light is killed.*)

—Golda.

GOLDA: Next time listen.

TV INTERVIEWER: I did. Thank you.

(*The TV pair leave, right;* LOU *comes from the rear, as* GOLDA *lights a cigarette.*)

LOU: At eleven, the military—

GOLDA: I'll be here.

LOU [BRIGHTLY]: —wish to know what to do next.

GOLDA: Win.

(LOU *leaves, left;* GOLDA *stands alone, heavy.*)

And that's what we've—given our lives to— Morris—

(*The lights change to memory,* GOLDA *goes into herself.*)

What is the price—

(*She waves her thoughts away with the smoke.*)

1928.

(MORRIS *in 1928 garb, carrying a package, stands in shadow at rear;* GOLDA *comes front as a Witness.*)

1928 we signed the Declaration of—

MORRIS: '48.

GOLDA [STOPS]: '48.

MORRIS: 1928 was your own declaration.

GOLDA [A PAUSE, NOT TURNING]: —we signed the Declaration of Independence. Which started, With trust in the Rock of Israel we—and already we couldn't agree, the rabbis demanded we say God and the left wouldn't sign to a rock, and B. G. spent half the day convincing everybody the Rock meant God *or* the people, and Sharef was waiting to rush the scroll to a bank-vault so it would last even if we didn't—from my window I saw four Egyptian Spitfires zoom in to bomb Tel Aviv—and in Washington we couldn't get it to the White House till we agreed even on a name for the state; but then B. G. read out the Declaration to us, very matter-of-fact till he came to, The State of Israel will be open to Jewish immigration and the ingathering of exiles, when his voice broke, and my turn to sign somebody behind me said, Why are you crying so, Goldie?—and in Washington they hurried the paper to the White House without a name, at the sentry-box there was a phone message for the courier, Israel, right there he wrote it in and took it inside. Midnight my phone rang, Goldie, are you listening, Truman has recognized us!—ten minutes after he got it; I always thought under different circumstances he could be Jewish.

(She gathers cigarettes and letter, turns back.)

And that's how after nineteen hundred years of exile we brought the state into being again.

MORRIS: Tell the first story.

GOLDA: What?

MORRIS: 1928. Politics you always—found a hiding place—

(GOLDA *walks away left, in a blind circle, as the small girl and boy come in night-clothes to stand on either side of* MORRIS; *sound begins, a scratchy record of Caruso singing, while* MORRIS *comes with the package and sits in the chair to unwrap it;* GOLDA *in the shadows behind him sees the children gazing.*)

GOLDA: Go to bed and keep warm, Sarile—

MORRIS: Today I was paid in cash, not scrip. So, being so unexpectedly a man of wealth, I bought something for the soul—

GOLDA: Menachem, for the last time, go to bed!

(*The children run off squealing, and* MORRIS *unwraps a lovely lampshade;* GOLDA *stares.*)

MORRIS: Lo and behold. You like it?

GOLDA [FLAT]: It's beautiful.

MORRIS [PAUSE]: You don't like it.

GOLDA: It's beautiful, it's beautiful.

MORRIS: No, it's—not beautiful, now. Goldie dear, the kerosene lamp is so ugly—

GOLDA: Turn the record off.

MORRIS: It's Caruso—

GOLDA: I almost killed a man today.

MORRIS: What?—Who?

GOLDA: Turn the record off!

(She herself turns abruptly, stands in the shadows, and sound stops; MORRIS sits with the lampshade, GOLDA paces in the shadows.)

Morris, I can't live the—way I—

MORRIS [QUIET]: Tell me about the man.

GOLDA: Nobody wants the scrip, you know that, twenty minutes I have to beg the butcher for half a pound of soup bones, bread and margarine yesterday the grocer wouldn't give me on credit, today—they go to bed hungry!—that grobber-jung downstairs was telling the milkman watch out for us he wouldn't get his money, I picked up a stick—shouting at him and *hitting* him, on the—

MORRIS: Really?

GOLDA: —on the head, on the head—

MORRIS: Was he hurt?

GOLDA: Of course he was hurt, if he didn't run so good he'd be down there yet. It's very beautiful, show it to Sara, she has a sore throat.

(A silence.)

I sound like my mother. It's not what I came to Palestine for.

MORRIS: Goldie dear, how much can a bookkeeper make?—times are very bad here—

GOLDA: Look, it's not money.

MORRIS: —in this paradise—

GOLDA: I was furious to start with, I came back from the
    nursery-yard—

MORRIS: So give it up.

GOLDA: Morris—

MORRIS: I didn't suggest you scrub the whole school's
    laundry—

GOLDA: I can't feed them, I'll *pay* the school? It's not
    the work either, I worked harder in the kibbutz—

MORRIS: Ah!—the blessed kibbutz—

GOLDA: —and was anyway thinking I should never have
    left—

MORRIS: I was sick!—I—

GOLDA: —sick of it—

MORRIS: —didn't ask to dig myself into a grave either—

GOLDA: —the worst mistake I made.

MORRIS: No, you made one before.

GOLDA: What?

MORRIS: You married me.

(A *silence.*)

GOLDA: Look. I'm going back to Party work.

(A *silence.*)

MORRIS: Someone invited you?

GOLDA: Yes.

MORRIS: Who?

GOLDA: I met somebody in Tel Aviv last week, the
    Histadrut needs a—

MORRIS: Who?

GOLDA: —secretary of the Women's Council; they're setting up farms to train immigrant girls in—

MORRIS: I thought you stopped seeing those people.

GOLDA [PAUSE]: I'll find a place in Tel Aviv, there's a— workers' house on Hayarkon—

MORRIS: I work in Jerusalem, Goldie.

GOLDA: —and you can come on weekends.

MORRIS: No. No.

GOLDA: Today I made up my mind.

MORRIS: Go, then. The children stay here.

GOLDA: You'll take them to the office?

MORRIS: You'll take them to the office?

GOLDA: I'll hire help. There's a school.

MORRIS [DAZED]: You—have it all calculated out. Money, work, politics—but it's them—

GOLDA [NOW THE LIONESS]: No, I've had enough!—

MORRIS: —all your Party cronies—

GOLDA: —so jealous of my work and friends—

MORRIS: —they steal you from me—

GOLDA: —four years I've given to two rooms here, the worst time of my life, I'm thirty years old, what's my head full of?—bills I can't pay, shoes are falling apart, Sara has a cough, my whole life is bargaining over two chicken-legs—I'm in Milwaukee!—other people like me for the things you hate, I have a mind of my own!—and what I came here for I won't live without.

MORRIS [SHAKY]: I followed you from Denver to this wasteland and you'll make me live alone here?

GOLDA: I get smaller every year.

MORRIS: You're—letting me down, Goldie—

GOLDA [FIERCE]: Who let who down?
MORRIS [PAUSE]: Yes.

(*He crushes the lampshade between his hands;* GOLDA *is stricken.*)

GOLDA: Oh, Morris—

(*She comes to the chair behind him; he shifts away from her touch.*)

MORRIS [IN TEARS]: I warned you, I wrote once didn't you ever think your Morris might lack the—indomitable will—Loving you is, you're a—thirty-year-old rock of Gibraltar—

(*He gets up, stands a moment—*)

I'll throw this out.

(*—and takes it toward the shadows;* GOLDA *is bent over the chair.*)

GOLDA: Morris, if I'm happier maybe it'll be better for everybody. I'll try harder, be a good wife, have the life I need—
MORRIS: We'll find out, I'll— Two things I know, Goldie—

(*He comes back, picks up the wrapping.*)

—you won't meet a man who doesn't let you down,
from your poppa with the boards on; the other—

(*He is on his way out, stops.*)

I love you for those things too. I'll never not love
you.

(*He goes out;* GOLDA *stands alone over the chair,
older.*)

GOLDA [SLOWLY]: What is the price?

(*Sound erupts—war, explosions and gunfire—as the
3RD and 4TH actors in khaki come in to her at
left.*)

4TH: Golda, it's a political decision, you have to make it.

(GOLDA *straightens, chain-lights a cigarette.*)

GOLDA: What?
3RD: We've pushed the Syrians off the Heights; do we
    push on?
4TH: Eytan can attack tomorrow at eleven with the 7th
    Brigade; Laner at one on the Damascus road—
GOLDA: What's political?
4TH: Invading Syria.

(*Pause.*)

3RD: There's a chance of Soviet intervention.

GOLDA: Yesterday in the Golan—

4TH: It was our best day, yes.

GOLDA: —we lost more boys than any day so far; you say best?

4TH: Tactically.

GOLDA: Tactically.

4TH: We can't turn to the Egyptians till we break the Syrian army; if we don't break it they'll absorb the Soviet stuff coming in. And we don't have the tanks you promised—

GOLDA: I talk to Dinitz in his sleep. Send the young to die, it's the—

4TH: You know Ran?—17th Brigade—

GOLDA: —the cruelest thing I have to do—

4TH: Wounded Sunday. His brother's in the hospital, another brother was killed with the Barak, I know the parents. I relieved him of his command.

(GOLDA *nods.*)

He refused to obey, said nobody makes my decisions for me, he's back fighting all bandaged up.

GOLDA [PAUSE]: But if I can't do it, get out and let somebody do it who can. —You have a complex about the Soviets—

3RD: Perhaps.

GOLDA: Perhaps. So. Let's push into Syria.

(*She turns left; the men leave up right.*)

3RD: God help us if she's wrong.

(GOLDA *hears, hesitates and trudges up to her office,
where* LOU *is gathering dirty dishes from the desk.*)

GOLDA: Leave them.

LOU: No, you hate a sloppy desk.

GOLDA: I'll wash them later.

LOU: My dear Prime Minister, there's a girl.

GOLDA [SITS]: They're my dishes. If this war ever ends,
every dish in my house I'll wash again. I miss it.

LOU: Yes, it is an interesting hobby.

GOLDA: If it ends.

(*She sits forward, face in hands.*)

Why did we take this job?

LOU: You said you would not accept without me.

GOLDA: You could have refused; we'd both be home
with our dishes.

LOU: I did.

GOLDA: I meant to leave after three months—

LOU: Well, you came to like it; and so did I.

GOLDA: I don't like it.

LOU: There is the power, dear lady.

GOLDA: Power. Wash a dish it's clean, that's power.

(LOU *goes out with the dirty dishes.*)

God help us if I'm wrong.

(*She is moveless a moment, then paws among
papers. From right the* 6TH *Witness—the* 2ND *actor,
a different role—comes to the chair.*)

6TH WITNESS: Golda?—I've been in the opposition for thirty years, she was nothing but a tough Party workhorse and never popular. Ran for mayor of Tel Aviv in '55 and couldn't get elected; retired in '66, too sick to work, and got 3 percent of the vote in a popularity poll; was made Prime Minister in '69 only as a stopgap—wasn't too sick, somebody said she suffers from psychosomatic health. Like Pavlov, say the word duty and the workhorse salivates.

(*He lights a small flame in the floor at center, rises.*)

She was always contentious. In London she walked out on Weizmann because he said she was irresponsible; for years she didn't talk to Ben-Gurion because he said she was corrupt.

GOLDA [NOT LOOKING UP]: Stupid and corrupt.

6TH WITNESS: And now she's Mother Israel. I'll give you Golda the politico in a nutshell: you're in a dark hall and at the end she's sitting in a light, the earth mother, sending out waves of protective warmth, and you can't resist, you throw yourself on her bosom and the next minute you're dead.

(*He takes the chair out right.*)

GOLDA [WAITS]: The last time someone threw himself on my bosom I'm too old to remember; they didn't act dead.

(*She rises, as* LOU *comes back with papers.*)

I want to cable Dinitz. Go public.
LOU [WRITES]: Go public.
GOLDA: Saturday.
LOU: Saturday.
GOLDA: Unless.
LOU: Unless—?
GOLDA: That's all.

(LOU *goes out;* GOLDA *comes heavily to the front of the desk.*)

I'll give you all of us in a nutshell: you're in a dark hall—

(*The lights go dark, the small flame burns on the floor.*)

—and the light isn't on me, it's our eternal flame to the six million Hitler killed. Yad Vashem. Yad vashem, it's from Isaiah, I will give you a memorial and a name; we're still trying to collect each name. The building's on a hill outside Jerusalem.

(*She comes down—*)

You walk up the Path of the Just, each tree named for a non-Jew who risked his life to save one of us; above is what looks like a smokestack—

(*—walks upstage—*)

—the memorial shaft, out of—heaps of ashes?—

(—*stands*—)

—and a plaque, Now and forever in memory of
those who died sanctifying the name of God;
further on—

(—*and turns down past the flame.*)

—is the Hall of Remembrance. Inside it's dark,
except for the flame. It takes a minute before you
see, on the floor is writing. Twenty-two names.
Buchenwald, Treblinka, Babi Yar, Auschwitz,
Theresienstadt-Terezin, Dachau, Bergen-Belsen—

(*A long moment of silence.*)

Nothing else. Israel?—stand here, everything in it
makes sense.

(*Slowly the lights begin to come back.*)

And outside down the steps for a few cents you
can buy a very good knish, because life goes on.

(*The lights rise, as five actors come down separately with chairs, eliminate the flame, and seat
themselves as around a circular table in cabinet
meeting; they include a* RELIGIOUS MINISTER *in
skullcap—the* 1ST *Witness, a different role.*)

2ND [IN KHAKI]: The Suez problem—

(*He waits for* GOLDA *to come sit, downstage, her back to us.*)

GOLDA: Talk, talk.

2ND: —is that our strength is speed and maneuver, and we're nailed down in a static war; they're sitting under an umbrella of missiles. The only way to break it up is cross the Canal.

RELIGIOUS MINISTER: You tried on the 8th.

4TH: No. Wait till they come out to attack, smash it, cross then.

GOLDA: Why should they come out?—I'd sit there under my umbrella—

2ND: They'll come out because their Syrian partner is screaming take the pressure off me.

1ST: What about supply routes?

2ND: The one we make.

3RD: One?

2ND: The one we make. We probed on the 8th between their Second and Third armies, and there's a chance to reach the Canal without a heavy battle.

(*He passes a photo.*)

Golda, this is the bridge.

GOLDA: Bridge?

1ST: The prize bridge.

2ND: The one Sharon will cross the Canal with. Two hundred yards long, it moves on rollers, tanks tow it; when it goes into the water it spans the Canal.

RELIGIOUS MINISTER: You base a crossing like that on a
    single supply route?

2ND: Give me two.

(*A pause.*)

GOLDA [HEAVILY]: A crossing is very risky.

2ND: Very. But if they come out from under the mis-
    siles, it's our chance.

(*A pause.*)

1ST [RISES]: We'll see how it goes in the next two days.

(*The meeting begins to break up; they remove
chairs.*)

GOLDA: I don't have an easy heart for it.

(*They stop.*)

4TH: Golda, there's no choice.

GOLDA: Syria, how are our losses?

1ST: We're bleeding out.

2ND: We're exhausted, Golda—fighting for a week
    against fresh reinforcements, no time to eat, boys
    fall asleep halfway into a sentence—

3RD: I said to Benni today we're hoping for more planes;
    he said, God knows if I'll have pilots to fly them.

(GOLDA *sits with bowed head; the* 4TH *lingers behind the others leaving.*)

4TH: Golda, we have two options. A crossing to end
    the war is one.

GOLDA: What's the other?

4TH: Settle for a cease-fire.

(*He walks out after the others; only the* RELIGIOUS
MINISTER *remains, and comes to* GOLDA *as she
rises.*)

RELIGIOUS MINISTER: I was visiting the wounded, Golda,
    do you know a soldier named—

(*He looks at a piece of paper.*)

Mordecai Stern?

GOLDA: Mordecai Stern.

RELIGIOUS MINISTER: Modke?

GOLDA: No.

RELIGIOUS MINISTER [WITH A FLOWER]: He sent you this,
    he was one of the Cyprus children—

GOLDA [TAKES IT]: Cyprus.

RELIGIOUS MINISTER: —he gave you some paper flowers
    there?

GOLDA [PAUSE]: I still have those flowers. Yes, give him
    my love.

(*The* RELIGIOUS MINISTER *opens his hands, help-
less.*)

RELIGIOUS MINISTER [THEN]: I'm sorry.

(*He goes out, with the chair;* GOLDA *stands alone, and the lights change to memory.*)

GOLDA: Modke. Modke.

(*Up right three children—boy, small girl, younger boy—in refugee rags stand silhouetted on the platform, gazing at* GOLDA; *down left, the lights next find a* BRITISH COMMANDANT—*the* 3RD *actor, a different role—waiting with a letter.*)

Cyprus—

COMMANDANT: Mrs. Myerson.

GOLDA: —where, after Hitler, the British ran a concentration camp for Jews—

COMMANDANT: Our White Paper limits immigration into Palestine.

GOLDA [TURNS]: —refugees sailing there by the thousands you stop in mid-ocean, and cage up on Cyprus—

COMMANDANT: We let them into Palestine by quota—

GOLDA: The very people you saved are now your prisoners.

COMMANDANT: My government has a hundred million Arabs to placate, Mrs. Myerson; now what do you expect of *me*?

GOLDA: To do what the letter says.

COMMANDANT: You are permitted seven hundred and fifty a month, you may select them.

GOLDA: The babies and orphans we have a list of; if I can—

COMMANDANT: There is no mention of orphans here.

GOLDA: If the Secretary's forgotten what he promised, I haven't; I'll—

COMMANDANT: He has not forgotten, he sent me a telegram, Beware of Mrs. Myerson. She is a formidable person.

GOLDA: How nice he remembers.

COMMANDANT: I will have you taken to the huts. There is a committee for each camp, and a committee of the committees; a talkative people. I suggest that you meet first with the committee of the committees—

(*He leaves, as the children come down—*)

GOLDA: Hello.

(*—to circle* GOLDA—)

I'm Goldie, what's your name?

(*—and mutely retreat up left to wait, gazing; meanwhile from left and right three* DP's *in rags come in—*)

I'm Goldie Myerson from the Agency—

(*—to nod and sit on the floor around her. Understudies come to fill out each group in turn.*)

I've come about the children. We know how many have died here—

1ST DP [LEVEL]: How many?

GOLDA: Forty-eight.

2ND DP: Forty-nine, today.

GOLDA [PAUSE]: It's the winter that worries us, we think they won't get through it. The doctors tell us there's dysentery in the huts—

2ND DP: There's no water.

GOLDA: —and an epidemic isn't out of the question.

1ST DP: So get us out.

GOLDA: Every last one—on the day we have a state. Tell me, are some of you due to leave?

3RD DP [A WOMAN]: I'm on the next month's quota.

GOLDA: You have children?

3RD DP: It's my one blessing. No.

GOLDA: Then it's you I came to ask. Will you let a child go in your place?

(*The Woman stands up; a silence.*)

3RD DP: It's—first in, first out—

GOLDA: The British will waive it, if the detainees do.

3RD DP: I'm nineteen months here, I'm sick myself, you want me to die here?

(*A silence; the* DP's *stand up, one after another.*)

1ST DP: This committee has no say on it. You'll have to go to each hut.

GOLDA: I'll begin in the morning.

(*The* DP's *move away, not leaving; the children come down, circling* GOLDA, *and the small girl beckons her to follow—*)

What's your name?

(*—to up right, where other* DP's *stand waiting;
the children retreat.*)

Good morning.

(*The* DP's *sit on the platform,* GOLDA *stands below.*)

Insult you I won't; we don't know what you've
been through. What camp were you in?
4TH DP [GIRL]: Bergen-Belsen.

(GOLDA *is reading her numbered arm, she pulls it
behind her—*)

No.

(*—and begins to sniffle.*)

5TH DP [PAUSE]: The officers'—girl.

(*The girl jumps up, turns to leave—*)

GOLDA: I promise you, in Eretz Israel, everything is new.

(*—and the girl stops.*)

It begins now.
4TH DP: How?
GOLDA: Let a child go.
5TH DP: Parents go with them?

GOLDA: How else?

4TH DP: So people who've waited a year for their quota stay, somebody with a child who came last week leaves?—that's what you're asking—

GOLDA: It's what I'm asking.

5TH DP: The huts have to vote.

GOLDA: You'll have a meeting?

4TH DP: Tomorrow.

GOLDA: Can I talk at it?

(The DP's break up, not leaving; the children come to lead GOLDA, the small girl taking her hand, down left—)

SMALL GIRL: Ruthie.

GOLDA: Thanks, Ruthie.

(—to other DP's, sitting down on the floor; the children back away.)

Good evening. You know what I'm—

6TH DP: It's all we've been talking since yesterday.

7TH DP: Maybe we'll disappoint you.

GOLDA: It's what they said in the Agency.

6TH DP: It'll take years to empty this camp.

GOLDA: No. You'll have a meeting?

7TH DP: Yes, tonight.

(The DP's stand, not leaving; the children come to lead GOLDA across down right—)

BOY: I'm Nahum.

GOLDA: So maybe you'll be a prophet too, they had courage, they didn't care if they got elected—

(—*where other* DP's *sit on the platform; the* 8TH, *a woman, rises.*)

Good afternoon—

8TH DP [SAVAGE]: I vote yes, you got my vote, now go away!

(*She thrusts past,* GOLDA *takes her elbow.*)

GOLDA: No, don't talk to me like that without a—

8TH DP: I *killed* my baby.

(*She breaks away, disappears among the others;* GOLDA *stares.*)

9TH DP [PAUSE]: She was hiding in a sewer with a group, the Nazis were above, the baby started crying—

(GOLDA *stops it with a hand.*)

GOLDA [THEN]: I know that story.

9TH DP: She smothered it.

1ST DP [CROSSING]: There's a mass meeting in the morning, we'll make a recommendation—

GOLDA: Look, I'm not asking you to stay here forever.

1ST DP: If you want to talk to it—

(*He leads her up right on the platform; all the* DP's *are below now, and* GOLDA *speaks to them as she walks.*)

GOLDA: We'll have a state. Someday we'll have a state.

(*She stands above them; they wait, scattered, listening.*)

You came from the DP camps of Germany, France —You remember in every camp schoolroom there was a map. Of Palestine. The children learned its geography, sang its songs, talked of arriving—And the teachers said, Without this map the children would lose hope.

Fifteen thousand children went into the death camp at Terezin, one hundred came out. If we lose the children, we lose the future.

No. No. If we lose the children we lose the children. It's up to you.

(*She comes down among them; they part to let her pass. The* 1ST DP *takes her down front.*)

1ST DP: We'll vote. You wait outside.

(*He leaves her, and returns to the crowd, motionless with backs to us.* GOLDA *sits on the ground, to wait; and the children come down with a bouquet of flowers.*)

YOUNGER BOY: Goldie?

(GOLDA *turns; he hands her the flowers, made of scraps of paper. After a moment* GOLDA *smells them.*)

SMALL GIRL: They're only paper.
GOLDA: Really?
BOY: There's no flowers here.
GOLDA: They're the realest flowers I ever saw.
SMALL GIRL: You could put perfume on them.
YOUNGER BOY [POINTS]: I made this one.
SMALL GIRL: I made this one and—
BOY: I made these three!
SMALL GIRL: —and this one—

(*A pause.*)

GOLDA: I'll always keep them.

(*The 1st DP comes back down to GOLDA.*)

1ST DP: They voted.
GOLDA: How?
1ST DP: Yes.
GOLDA [FINALLY]: I knew they would.

(*She gets up; the DP's walk off, in all directions, and GOLDA reaches to stop the younger boy.*)

YOUNGER BOY: I'm Mordecai Stern. Modke.

(*He turns, and runs out after the others; GOLDA is alone.*)

GOLDA: Modke.—Choose life.

(*She sets the flowers carefully on the ground, and walks to her desk, to sit. She finds a cigarette and*

tries to light it, but is trembling so her fingers drop
it. She gets it lit and picks up her phone, as the
5TH *actor comes down right to pick up his.*)

Simcha.

5TH: Here.

GOLDA: You're seeing Kissinger tonight.

5TH: Yes, very late.

GOLDA: I have a message for him.

5TH: Yes?

GOLDA: Tell him we—Ask him—See if he can get us a
     cease-fire.

5TH: What?

GOLDA: In place.

5TH: What!

GOLDA: Try for a cease-fire in place.

5TH: It means we've lost! The cabinet really wants it?

GOLDA: Not yet.

5TH: Golda. What happened?

GOLDA: The resources to continue we don't have. Such
     losses, men, equipment, if we try to cross the
     Canal and bog down? The casualties, the casual-
     ties—

5TH: Ah.

GOLDA: The casualties are—hard to bear—

5TH: I'll tell Kissinger tonight, it's a gruesome message.

GOLDA: Tell him. It's too hard—

(*She puts the phone down.*)

—to bear so much death.

(*Lights change to memory as the* 5TH *actor leaves; sound begins, solo cello playing the Bach saraband, and* GOLDA *sees up right a small group of mourners,* SARILE *and* MENACHEM *from the garden scene, a Rabbi, one or two others, who come down to the flowers. They conduct a brief ceremony—the Rabbi reads a Hebrew prayer aloud,* MENACHEM *joins him in a responsory—and when it is over, sound dies away. All but the family walk slowly off, up right.*)

I was away when it happened—

MENACHEM: Always.

GOLDA [PAUSE]: What was he doing in my house that day?

SARILE: Sitting there, momma.

MENACHEM: Often, didn't you know?

SARILE: People who came for you would find him, sitting.

GOLDA: Yes. I knew.

MENACHEM: So death found him, sitting there.

SARILE: What did he think, sitting alone like that for hours?

(*She stands a moment, turns, walks out up right.*)

GOLDA: What I'm thinking now.

(MENACHEM *squats.*)

MENACHEM: Morris Myerson. Born, Velish, 1894; died, Tel Aviv, 1951. Loved music, brought with him from Milwaukee all those breakable old records,

Galli-Curci, Caruso, Tetrazzini. Loved language, read the poets, Joyce, Proust. And Freud, loved knowledge; went partners with a friend to buy the Encyclopedia Britannica, the survivor to own the books; always gave me books as a present. Didn't think much of politics, loved the things of the— mind, spirit?—he was a strange kind of bookkeeper. I miss him.

(MENACHEM *rises, walks out up right.*)

GOLDA [ALONE]: Oh, Morris. The best man I knew, such a price I made *you* pay. We didn't live the life we intended. Yes, we have the state; it doesn't keep people from dying.

(*She remains at her desk; down left the* 7TH *Witness—the* 4TH *actor, a different role—comes on, to pick up the flowers.*)

7TH WITNESS: Golda, yes, I was at the UN with her when she was making the speeches. Eban would write the first draft, she'd correct it—Maimonides? take out Maimonides, everybody'll laugh at me— but the best speech she made there was the day she put the text down and just talked, to the Arabs.

She said, Look, it's the tenth anniversary of Israel. The only way you recognize us is in trying to wipe us out. Israel is here. Our greatest grief is the lack of peace with our neighbors. What's the use of

pretending Israel isn't here?—does hate for us make
one child in your country happier? does it turn
one hovel into a house? The deserts are in need
of water, not bombers. Wouldn't it be better to
wipe out poverty, illiteracy, disease?—can't we
build a future for the Middle East together?

They didn't look up.

(*He goes off left with the flowers; down right the
5TH actor hurries in, snatches up his phone.*)

5TH: Golda, Golda, Golda.

(*The phone on* GOLDA's *desk rings once, twice—*)

Golda!—Lou, Lior, anyone—

(*—till* GOLDA *picks it up.*)

GOLDA: Yes.
5TH: Golda. Kissinger surprised me, Don't ask for a
cease-fire now—
GOLDA: What?
5TH: He said, You don't ask for a cease-fire when your
back is to the enemy.

(GOLDA *hits her fist on the desk.*)

GOLDA: *Then let him send us help!*
5TH: It's on the way.

(*Silence.*)

It's on the way! They're turning the depots inside out, Europe, here, they'll replace everything—the C-5's are airborne, a fleet of them, there'll be fourteen Phantoms there by Monday—

(GOLDA *begins to weep.*)

Golda?
GOLDA: Simcha.
5TH: Yes?
GOLDA: Thank you.
5TH: Anytime.

(*Sound comes in, a distant jet-roar growing overhead, as* GOLDA *and the* 5TH *actor hang up, and the entire stage goes sky-blue while the roar passes overhead—then another, then another; the roar is ear-splitting.*)

(*During it actors run onstage from all directions, gazing up, mute.*)

(*When the roar subsides, they go off; the* 1ST *and* 2ND *actors in khaki enter down right.*)

1ST: Golda!—the Egyptians are moving their armor—
GOLDA [TURNS]: To attack.
1ST: —they're out from under their missiles—
2ND: The bridge will be ready.
1ST: It must be in the water tomorrow night—
2ND: We assembled it five days ago.
1ST: —the entire time-table is built on that assumption—

GOLDA [COMES DOWN]: Where is it now?

2ND: At Yukon, ten miles from the Canal.

1ST: Sharon will lead—paratroopers, to knock out missiles in range of the bridge—

2ND: We launch a holding attack at five, secure the corridor, tow the bridge in.

GOLDA: Use good chains.

(*The men turn to leave.*)

Chaim. I'll get the cabinet together, we'll wait for news—

2ND: I'll phone it in.

(*They go out, up right.*)

GOLDA [ALONE]: Gamble, with more lives, on one drive to end the war—

(*She turns left, lights changing to night; LOU is entering with a tray of coffee.*)

I'll do that. Get the Foreign Ministry, make sure Eban understands he's playing for time.

LOU: He does; I'll check it.

(*GOLDA turns down right, where cabinet ministers —the 3RD, 4TH and 5TH actors, in different roles, and the RELIGIOUS MINISTER—come down with chairs to the low platform, and settle down for a waiting session.*)

GOLDA [WITH TRAY]: All week I've thought about my life; I began with the brotherhood of man, and end up as hostess of a war—

(LOU *goes up to the office phone; and* GOLDA *hands out coffee.*)

1ST MINISTER: How soon will they cross?
GOLDA: Any minute.
2ND MINISTER: What did you wire Nixon?
GOLDA: When we win we'll have you in mind.
RELIGIOUS MINISTER: It's not what I will have in mind.
3RD MINISTER: Who then?—I know, a higher official—
RELIGIOUS MINISTER: My boy.
GOLDA: Where is he?
RELIGIOUS MINISTER: In the 7th Battalion—with Sharon.
GOLDA: Well. He has a brave commander.
RELIGIOUS MINISTER: It's what worries me.

(*The phone down right rings;* GOLDA *crosses to pick it up and converses inaudibly as sound comes in, gunfire and three half-intelligible voices on radio crackling—*)

—*Matt here, Matt here.*
—*Matt, yes.*
—*Where the fuck are my boats?*
—*Boats.*
—*I was promised sixty inflatable boats this morning at ten o'clock—*
—*Just a minute.*
—*I moved out at 4:30, I'm in the goddamnedest*

traffic jam you ever saw, no boats—

—They're coming in from Tasa.

—Tasa?

*—They're at the wrong rendezvous, when will you
be in the yard?*

*—Never, it's taken me two hours to go three
miles—*

—They'll be waiting for you in the yard—

(—till GOLDA *hangs up.)*

1ST MINISTER: So?

GOLDA [THEN]: It looks good. They're widening the corridor, very little resistance. Amnon says they're
collapsing.

2ND MINISTER: Oh, marvellous—

*(They jump up, hug each other with exclamations
—"Finally . . . now uncross your fingers . . . it's
time, it's time! . . . I'll sleep tonight. . . ."—but*
GOLDA *sits again.)*

2ND MINISTER: Did they cross yet?

GOLDA: Not yet. It's been postponed.

3RD MINISTER: Till when?

GOLDA: Two hours.

RELIGIOUS MINISTER: Is anything wrong?

GOLDA: Just the supply route, they're making sure.

3RD MINISTER: Be patient.

RELIGIOUS MINISTER [SMILES]: I'm nervous—

3RD MINISTER: Have faith.

(*All quiet down.*)

(*They sit in different chairs, one reads a newspaper, some stand conversing, all smoke, one or two take more coffee.*)

1ST MINISTER: I'm smoking too much.
2ND MINISTER: It's a national disease.
1ST MINISTER: Why?—I don't even like it.
2ND MINISTER: We feel insecure—
3RD MINISTER: We are insecure.

(GOLDA *spies* LOU *returning with a paper bag, gets up to meet her, apart.*)

GOLDA: It's all right about Eban?
LOU: He will hold them spellbound for a week. What is transpiring here?
GOLDA [PAUSE]: The bridge is stuck.

(LOU *waits;* GOLDA *goes up to the office, sits. The group settles in different chairs; two men exchange newspapers, one works on a chess problem;* LOU *collects coffee cups, distributes food.*)

1ST MINISTER: It's terrible waiting like this.
3RD MINISTER: Yes, if there was anything we could do—besides wait—
RELIGIOUS MINISTER [STANDS]: There is. I should have, before—
1ST MINISTER: Where are you going?

(*The* RELIGIOUS MINISTER *walks out, up right.*)

2ND MINISTER: Downstairs.

3RD MINISTER: To the w.c.

2ND MINISTER: To the synagogue.—Here's a riddle, what's the difference between a w.c. and a synagogue?

3RD MINISTER: I don't know.

2ND MINISTER: Don't come to my synagogue.

3RD MINISTER [STARES]: You're getting very tired.

2ND MINISTER: Yes.

(GOLDA *at her desk picks up the phone; sound comes in as she converses, great explosions and many voices on radio crackling—*)

—*The Akavish road is open.*

—*No, it's not, goddamit! They came out of their holes and closed it—*

—*Sir, a section is broken down.*

—*Where are you?*

—*Sharon, Sharon!*

—*I can't evacuate casualties—*

—*7th Battalion.*

—*How long to repair?*

—*Just west of the Chinese Farm—*

—*Sharon here.*

—*Two hours, three hours, we're under artillery fire, sir—*

—*Have you infantry to comb the area?*

—*What've they got behind you?*

—*I have infantry, don't know that it's enough—*

—*Tank, missile, bazooka fire*—

—*Matt here, Matt here*—

—*7th Battalion, I'm down to one-third strength*—

—*Nathan!*

—*We're in the middle of a fucking center here!
Trucks, guns, dug-in tanks, radar*—

—*Matt here—Sharon!*

—*Nathan, all my tanks are out.*

—*ambulances, thousands of troops*—

—*I've got six half-tracks cut off, I'm moving in on
foot*—

—*Sharon here.*

—*Matt here, I'm in the yard with my boats and
tanks, I've got rafts for thirty tanks*—

—*Move out.*

—*I'm under shelling*—

—*Move out, move out!*

—*Everything's on fire, it's all hell burning up*—

(—*but the roar of explosions drown out all the
voices;* GOLDA *hangs up, comes down to the group.*)

1ST MINISTER: What's the word, Golda?

GOLDA: Our boys are in trouble.

3RD MINISTER: They weren't collapsing.

GOLDA: No. It's very heavy fighting. Very heavy.

(*She sits; abruptly then—*)

The worst fighting of the war, they said it was all
hell on fire there.

1ST MINISTER: Did they say how many killed?

GOLDA [HARSH]: They can't stop to count the dead!—
    hundreds, hundreds, they're fighting for the cross-
    roads behind them—
3RD MINISTER: Is the bridge across yet?
GOLDA: Not yet.

(*She sits again; the* RELIGIOUS MINISTER *returns.*)

It's broken down.

2ND MINISTER: What?
GOLDA [BITTERLY]: It's broken down, they were towing
    it, they're trying to fix it under artillery fire, the
    man got a prize for the bridge, it doesn't work.
2ND MINISTER: Broken down.
GOLDA: They'll fix it.
1ST MINISTER: How long will it take, did they say?
GOLDA: Three hours.
RELIGIOUS MINISTER: Did you hear any word of the 7th
    Battalion?
GOLDA [PAUSE]: No.
1ST MINISTER: Three hours.
3RD MINISTER: Be patient. You're not fighting.
1ST MINISTER: I'd go home to sleep, but I won't sleep.
3RD MINISTER: Be patient.—I'll jump out of my skin—

(*A silence.*)

GOLDA: They're in the fighting, of course.
RELIGIOUS MINISTER: Of course.
GOLDA: That's as much as I know.

(*The phone down right rings, she picks it up; the others wait.*)

Yes? . . . Yes. . . . Yes.

(*She puts the phone down. A silence.*)

I'm sorry. You've sat up for nothing—
2ND MINISTER: They didn't get the bridge over?
GOLDA: No. Not until tomorrow, maybe later.
3RD MINISTER: Then there's no surprise.
GOLDA: No.
1ST MINISTER: Are we winning?—losing?
GOLDA: Killing and dying. Not clear, nobody knows, it
    could be a terrible setback.

(*She sits again, lights a cigarette; after a moment the others stir.*)

1ST MINISTER: It's very late—

(*They straggle out up right, except the* RELIGIOUS MINISTER, *who does not get up; the* 3RD MINISTER *waits for him.*)

LOU [PASSING]: I will be in the office.

(GOLDA *nods;* LOU *goes off, up left.*)

3RD MINISTER: Come.
RELIGIOUS MINISTER: It's a suffering world, Golda.
GOLDA [PAUSE]: Why?

RELIGIOUS MINISTER [OPENS HIS HANDS]: God's will.

GOLDA: It's a question I asked the Pope; he said man's.

RELIGIOUS MINISTER: Man's?

GOLDA: Man's will, the origin of all evil, you Zionists force your will, the Arabs force theirs, neither is God's will, and suffering comes. What he calls will, I call the dybbuk; and Israel *was* born of Zionist will. So it's my fault, the world.

RELIGIOUS MINISTER: What did you answer?

GOLDA: I said, you remind me of my husband.

3RD MINISTER: Did you really?

GOLDA: No; I thought of it afterwards. And I didn't say that ever since one of our young Rabbis said turn the other cheek the most obedient Christians in the world have been the Jews, and it took us into the gas-chambers—That was God's will?

RELIGIOUS MINISTER: How can I think so?

GOLDA: Yes, we *willed* this state into being, so we could live. Some die, others live.

3RD MINISTER [PAUSE]: Come.

(*He goes out; the* RELIGIOUS MINISTER *stays. Another silence.*)

RELIGIOUS MINISTER: It's not as much as you know. Is it?

GOLDA: What?

RELIGIOUS MINISTER: About my son's battalion.

(*He waits; she does not look at him.*)

Tell me, tell me, Golda.

GOLDA: I heard nothing about names.

RELIGIOUS MINISTER: Numbers.

GOLDA: The 7th Battalion is down to one-third strength.

(They sit unmoving; and presently the RELIGIOUS MINISTER *begins to weep, with closed eyes, to himself.)*

GOLDA: It was a gamble. Some die, others live, was anything in this world ever changed except by some who die for it? If there's a God—

RELIGIOUS MINISTER: There is.

GOLDA: —then he made the dybbuk too, and the dream, and the dying for it.

RELIGIOUS MINISTER: I know there is.—Dying isn't what it seems, Golda, but it hurts.

GOLDA: No, living hurts. I think now, this state doesn't give security. It gives us something better.

RELIGIOUS MINISTER: What?

GOLDA: Opportunities. To be. To do, to hurt, to gamble, lose or win, and die for something better; maybe that's God's will?—I hope your boy lives.

(The RELIGIOUS MINISTER *stands, starts out, then comes back behind* GOLDA.*)*

RELIGIOUS MINISTER: In the wilderness, when the children of Israel fought, Moses all day held up the rod of God in his hand; and Israel prevailed. But his arms grew tired.

GOLDA: Yes.

RELIGIOUS MINISTER: So his brothers held up his arms,

and his hands were steady until the going down
of the sun.—Good night, Golda.

(*He goes out.*)

(GOLDA *sits alone a moment, then tries to lift her
arms, like Moses, and cannot. She gets up, and
trudges to the steps down left.*)

(*The phone in the office rings, and* LOU *answers it.*
GOLDA *climbs the steps;* LOU *waits, holding the
phone out.*)

LOU: Sharon is across.
GOLDA [INCREDULOUS]: How?
LOU: On rafts.
GOLDA: Rafts?
LOU: He didn't wait for the bridge.

(GOLDA *stands on the top step, not moving, then
does lift her arms—*)

GOLDA: Opportunities—

(*—as the lights rise to daylight at center; and* GOLDA
walks down into it.)

At this hour, our forces are operating on the west
bank of the Canal.

(*There is shouting, and all the actors run in, jubi-
lant, cheering, hugging each other;* GOLDA *quiets it
with a hand.*)

The tide has turned. I can't say more, there's still fighting to be done.

(*She turns to us.*)

There's still fighting to be done, is that news? Security, no, in all our lives we've had only a choice of dangers. And we didn't make a paradise. But—

(*The entire cast is in, standing or sitting, listening; the small flame burns on the floor.*)

—seventy years ago in Kiev my father nailed up boards against a pogrom; I can still hear the hammer. And to come in one lifetime all the way from the sound of that hammer to life in a state of our own, where we can defend our children, and be free, and take in every brother in the world who wants to come home—what more can a Jew ask?

Our lives have been blessed, whatever the price.

(SARILE *and* MENACHEM *enter last, down right.*)

Opportunities, opportunities, and you'll want younger blood. I don't blame you, I want some myself.

(*She turns right to leave, sees* SARILE.)

SARILE: Momma.
GOLDA [PAUSE]: I didn't do very well by my children.

SARILE: Momma—

MENACHEM: It's all right.

GOLDA: You didn't wish many times you had a different
mother?

SARILE: Often, but—never—

(MENACHEM *takes* GOLDA's *hand. Down left the*
1ST *Witness is on a step.*)

1ST WITNESS: Golda?—no more stories, seventy-five years
won't go into two hours—

GOLDA: And the time to say goodbye isn't far off.

(*She looks around as the actors starts to leave,*
but turns back to us.)

One word more—the best—

(*She says it to the audience, face by face—*)

Shalom. Shalom. Shalom. Shalom. Shalom. Shalom—

(*—until the lights lose her.*)

William Gibson

has published poetry, plays, fiction, and
autobiography; he is co-author with Margaret
Brenman, a psychoanalyst, of two grown
sons.

WITHDRAWN